MUSICAL
TRUTH

About the Author

Jeffrey Boakye is a writer, teacher and music enthusiast originally from Brixton, London. His books include, *Hold Tight* and *Black, Listed*. He is also the co-author of *What is Masculinity? Why Does it Matter? And Other Big Questions*. Jeffrey has taught English in secondary schools and sixth form colleges since 2007. He lives in East Yorkshire with his wife and two sons.

About the Illustrator

Ngadi Smart is an award-winning Sierra Leonean visual artist and designer based between London (UK) and Abidjan (Côte d'Ivoire), who specialises in illustration and photography. She has illustrated for *The Atlantic*, *Time Out London*, *The Guardian* and Eastpak, as well as for publishing houses. Ngadi won the 2020 FAB Prize for illustration.

FABER has published children's books since 1929. T. S. Eliot's *Old Possum's Book of Practical Cats* and Ted Hughes's *The Iron Man* were among the first. Our catalogue at the time said that 'it is by reading such books that children learn the difference between the shoddy and the genuine'. We still believe in the power of reading to transform children's lives. All our books are chosen with the express intention of growing a love of reading, a thirst for knowledge and to cultivate empathy. We pride ourselves on responsible editing. Last but not least, we believe in kind and inclusive books in which all children feel represented and important.

First published in the UK in 2021
by Faber & Faber Limited
Bloomsbury House, 74–77 Great Russell Street
London, WC1B 3DA
faberchildrens.co.uk

Typeset by M Rules in Mr Eaves
This font has been specially chosen to support reading
The chapter fonts have been selected to match those used by the artists themselves

Printed and bound by CPI Group (UK) Ltd, Croydon, CR0 4YY

A CIP record for this book
is available from the British Library

ISBN 978–0–571–36648–4

2 4 6 8 10 9 7 5 3 1

MUSICAL TRUTH

A Musical History of Modern Black Britain in 28 Songs

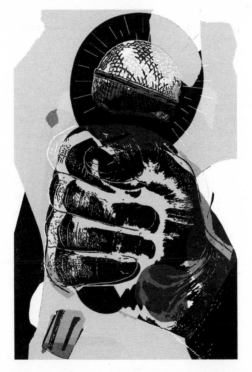

JEFFREY BOAKYE
Illustrated by Ngadi Smart

faber

For my two sons, all my nieces and nephews, and every child experiencing the world through music for the first time. Happy listening.

Playlist

Listen to the songs on our YouTube playlist at
musicaltruthplaylist.co.uk.

Hello.

Let me introduce myself.

My name is Jeffrey. I'm a teacher and a writer, and I was born in 1982, which might sound like a long time ago, even though it really isn't. It won't come as a surprise to you to hear that I haven't always been a teacher, or a writer. For much of my life, before I was an adult, I have been a kid growing up, exploring the world around me and trying to figure out what's going on.

Music has been a big part of this. Music opened my ears to a whole world beyond where I grew up, in a place called Brixton, in London. I've travelled the world through speakers and headphones, listening to sounds and stories from far and wide. I've always loved music and the way it can make your heart jump, or slow down, or skip a beat with excitement. I also love the way that you can be transported into the past, just by hearing songs that were made years before you were born.

I'm black. My parents were born in Ghana, west Africa, but they came over to the UK to have me after moving away from their home country. For me, being black means being Ghanaian and African, but it also means being part of a global family of other black people. Again, music is a key part of my identity as a black person. A lot of the music I listen to can be classified as 'black music' – made by black people and part of different black cultures.

I wrote this book because I feel deeply connected to black culture and black history, not just in Britain and Ghana, but all over the world and throughout history. Music has been my gateway to stories I have never lived through and people I have never met. I hope that this book will introduce songs that do the same thing for you.

Jeffrey Boakye

Introduction

From early on in all our lives, we learn history. Our own history, and the history of the world around us. Sometimes it's in a classroom, sometimes from the TV, or it might be from your parents, grandparents, aunts or uncles who won't stop telling you about what it was like when they were young, with phrases like 'I remember the time when . . .'

But these stories are important. They can show us what happened in the past, help us work out what life was like before we were born, and, if we pay enough attention, they can even help us understand what might happen in the future.

You might have learned about the Victorians, the Romans, the Egyptians . . . who knows. But what about the untold stories? What about the people who don't end up in textbooks and exam papers?

This book is going to open up a few of these stories and give you a few more pieces of the puzzle. It's going to take us on a journey through black British history, exploring how black culture has developed over time and influenced British society along the way, and we're going to do this through a selection of songs. Why songs? Because music is powerful. Music is life. Music can carry the stories of history like a message in a bottle.

And it can also do three very important things.

Music can be a *celebration*.

Music can be a way of talking about *oppression*.

Music can be a type of *resistance*.

For me personally, music has done all of this and much, much more. Ever since I was a child, I have loved exploring worlds outside of my home through songs and lyrics. Even before I owned any music of my own, I would listen to the radio or songs that were being played at parties and lose myself in sounds and rhythm. Music has always had a powerful impact on my life. Reggae and soul could calm me down while hiphop and dancehall could make my heart start racing. I would dance for hours with my siblings and cousins, lost in the joy that music can bring. That's the power of music.

When I was a kid, I remember playing my dad's old records on his huge stereo system, being introduced to funk, disco, jazz and Ghanaian highlife. I remember recording songs off the radio on my tape deck with my two older sisters, getting excited to hear the latest hits from our local station. I remember getting my first Walkman cassette player and listening to music on my own massive headphones, losing myself in the sounds of American hiphop, Jamaican dancehall and all sorts of sounds from the UK. I remember writing down song lyrics that I didn't even understand and reciting them to my friends in the playground. My whole life has beaten to the pulse of black music, and I'm telling you right now: we can learn a lot by looking at the world through a musical lens.

In this book, we'll explore songs from the global black community that do all of these things, sometimes all at once. We'll calypso through the 1940s and see reggae bounce its way into the 1980s. We'll catch soulful grooves in the 1990s and rap our way into the new millennium. We'll see UK garage step up the tempo on the dancefloor and eventually join grime on the rooftops of east London, in the early 2000s.

Get ready to travel the whole world on the sounds of the past and keep it moving right up to the present. We'll meet groundbreaking musicians whose songs have changed the world, and then we'll see one of the biggest black British superstars kicking up a storm(zy) in the here and now. Phew.

Welcome to *Musical Truth: A Musical History of Modern Black Britain in 28 Songs*.

You ready? Let's go.

Welcome to the British Empire

Now, before we really get going, we'll need to understand what is meant by something called the British Empire.

It's not that difficult. An empire is basically a collection of places that are owned and controlled, or 'colonised', by one powerful country. Not long ago, Britain had a huge empire that spread all over the world. It was so huge that people used to say, 'The sun never sets on the British Empire.' This is just a clever way of saying that the empire included so many countries across so many time zones, it was always daytime somewhere in a British-controlled country.

The British Empire was a system that allowed a very small country, Britain, to rule over huge chunks of the globe. Another name for it is British *imperialism*, and imperialism is great if you want to be in charge of everything (and don't really care about the people who were there before you). Have you ever wondered how and why English became one of the most widely spoken languages in the world, despite England being just one patch of a tiny island? It's because English is the language of the British Empire. If, let's say, France had built an empire that was as powerful as Britain's, then *on parlerait tous français maintenant* (we'd all be speaking French right now).

At one point, just before the First World War, the British Empire controlled more than 410 million people – across huge parts of Europe, America, Australia, Asia and Africa. This was nearly a quarter of everyone on the planet at the time. That's major. If you controlled nearly a quarter of the kids at your school right now, you'd probably be as powerful as the headteacher.

From this starting point, we can begin to understand how black people, originating from the continent of Africa, came to find themselves part of the British Empire. Eventually, millions of black people (like me) would even become British citizens, born in Britain, and would call it home.

The legacy of empire

Now, I couldn't really call this book *Musical Truth* without exposing a few truths along the way. This next bit is all about one of the biggest lies in British history, a lie told directly by the government.

After the Second World War, Britain found its empire starting to slow down and crumble. A number of its colonies were beginning to win their independence, which meant that the sun *was* finally beginning to set on the British Empire. The USA had been the first colony to gain independence from Britain all the way back in 1776, followed by Canada in 1867, Australia in 1901, Afghanistan in 1919, Egypt in 1922 and New Zealand in 1931. But it wasn't until after 1945 that other colonies (mainly in Africa and Asia) began to be free of British rule.

Times were changing. It was becoming clear that one country having complete control over lots of other countries was not a fair or modern way of doing things. It may seem obvious now that countries should have control over themselves, but in the 1940s a lot of our world was still controlled by Britain.

And the British Empire could be incredibly dangerous.

When countries tried to revolt against British imperial rule, they were often met with violent acts of control and terrorism by the British authorities. Here are some examples.

In Kenya (a name given to the territory by the British Empire after the tallest mountain in the country), hundreds and thousands of innocent people were forced to work without payment as slaves, imprisoned, tortured and brutally killed in mass executions.

In India during the 1870s, famines were made worse when the British Empire's rulers decided to increase exports of food from the country while its people literally starved to death. The money from these exports went straight back into the British economy.

Elsewhere, Britain was responsible for running concentration camps – such as in South Africa during the Boer War between 1899 and 1902. Tens of thousands of people died in these camps, often from disease or hunger. Many were children. Elsewhere, those in charge of the empire were responsible for carrying out massacres in order to conquer new territories, ignoring famines and profiting from the slave trade. Because Britain had such a powerful navy and a history of travelling around the world on great ships, it was very often British ships that carried slaves across the seas.

Many British people became wealthy off the back of the slave trade, setting up banks and other businesses that still exist today.

All of these actions were crimes against humanity.

British politicians knew this and didn't want to go into the second half of the twentieth century with the ghosts of the country's colonial past out on show for everyone to see. So they set about hiding evidence, like a criminal covering up their tracks. First, they changed the name of the 'Colonial Office' to the less imperial-sounding 'Foreign Office', which still exists to this day. Then they destroyed the evidence. Files that revealed the crimes of the empire were burned, buried and even dumped at sea. This process was known as Operation Legacy, a massive cover-up that is not usually taught in British schools. The dictionary tells us that 'legacy' means something that is left behind, usually after someone or something dies. In the 1940s, Britain was looking back at an incredibly dark past, but the government didn't want to look bad as it went into the future. The big question is: how can anyone really go forward without owning up to what they have done before?

As we continue looking at and listening to the history of black Britain, keep an eye out for the legacy of the British Empire.

'London Is the Place for Me'

Lord Kitchener (1948)

OK, so before we get on to the first song, there are a few things I want to tell you about the Caribbean. It's a part of the world that includes a collection of small islands that have had a big impact on British culture. And if we go back far enough, we'll see that it has a lot to do with sugar. But it's not a sweet story. And it started hundreds of years ago.

Back in the eighteenth century, it was discovered that Caribbean islands such as Jamaica and Barbados were perfect places to grow sugar crops. At the time, demand for sugar in Europe was increasing dramatically. Everyone loved the stuff, which meant that European landowners were keen to grow as much sugar as possible. Not wanting to be left out, Britain started to invest heavily in the sugar business.

At this point, Britain had already taken control over a number of Caribbean islands by sending people to settle there and colonise them. Barbados was taken in 1625 and Jamaica in 1655. By the eighteenth century, the British economy was relying on its Caribbean colonies to grow and sell sugar for profit. To do so, British traders needed workers. And the way they found workers was to sail to west Africa, force people away from their homes, pack them on ships and sail them to the Caribbean, where they were bought by British sugar plantation owners. They became enslaved.

It was a time of great cruelty and suffering, during which white Europeans forced black Africans to work, for free. And if these Africans resisted, they were killed. Let's stop and think about that for a second. Can you imagine being taken from your family, your friends, your home, tied up in shackles and sent on a ship filled to every last inch with up to six hundred other slaves for almost three months, to a new continent thousands of miles away? If you survived that awful journey, can you then imagine being sold to a plantation owner, before being forced to work for free? Suffering beatings, seeing death, seeing killings? For the rest of your life.

Those who survived this harsh life had children of their own, born into slavery, and the cycle continued over and over until slavery was eventually abolished. You've probably heard about William Wilberforce, who is heralded as the British man who abolished slavery – an abolitionist. In reality, black slave rebellions, black British abolitionists and white British workers, alongside white abolitionists like Wilberforce, *all* worked to abolish the slave trade in Britain, in 1807. (Slavery itself would not be made illegal in Britain until 1838.) Then, the descendants of enslaved African people would go on to form communities in the British West Indies, where they lived for generations.

And when I say the 'West Indies', did you realise these countries are nowhere near India? The West Indies – countries like Jamaica, Barbados, Trinidad and Haiti – got given that name because when European sailors first went there, they got confused, and wrongly thought that they were somewhere near India!

Many of these 'West Indians' who grew up under the British Empire saw Britain as a home they had never visited. They were taught that Britain was the so-called 'mother country', like a parent who ruled them from across the ocean. They were also told that they could one day travel to Britain, where they would be welcomed by British people.

In 1948, this dream seemed to come true when the British parliament passed the British Nationality Act. This new law meant that anyone who was part of the British Empire was allowed to become a British citizen, including all those Caribbean men, women and children who thought of

Britain as their mother country. The British government was encouraging them to come to the UK to do jobs that needed doing after the Second World War. For many people from the Caribbean, Britain had always seemed to be a great nation offering endless possibilities, and when faced with job shortages or fewer opportunities in smaller countries like Jamaica, many men and women took the chance of a better life.

But the Caribbean is a long way from the UK, and there weren't jet aeroplanes to take people from their home countries to the mother country, so how did they get there? Well, in 1948 a ship called the *Empire Windrush* carried over a thousand paying passengers from different parts of the world all the way to Britain. Five hundred and thirty-nine of them were from Jamaica, the largest Caribbean island. These travellers and those who followed them became known as the 'Windrush generation', one of the most famous groups of Caribbeans to settle in the UK, establishing black communities that still exist today.

So what's all this got to do with music, and this song by someone called Kitchener? Well, if you haven't ever been to the Caribbean, then close your eyes and this song will take you straight there. It's called calypso, and it's a rhythmic type of music originating from Trinidad in the nineteenth century. It's somehow bouncy and laid-back at the same time, and when you hear it, you're suddenly on the beach squinting up at clear blue skies while a soft breeze cools you down.

Now, during the First World War, there was a famous British army officer called Lord Kitchener – but he didn't make calypso music, so don't worry about him. There's another Lord Kitchener, a man from Trinidad, who actually did make calypso music, and that's the one we're going to focus on. His real name was Aldwyn Roberts, and he was nicknamed after the earlier Lord Kitchener. It's very interesting that he chose a stage name that seemed to celebrate the British Empire. It shows how proud many black people were of Britain, even if they had never been there.

All of these facts are important, but the most important fact is that Aldwyn 'Lord Kitchener' Roberts was a passenger on board the *Empire Windrush*.

Lord Kitchener's song 'London Is the Place for Me' perfectly captures the optimism that West Indians coming to the UK felt in 1948. It's happy and fun and light-hearted, with a quiet innocence about how great London will be when the passengers get there. It even starts off with the sound of Big Ben chiming happily in the breeze, before you hear lyrics about how lovely London is and how the people of England will make you feel like a millionaire.

In reality, black people arriving in Britain faced overcrowded living conditions, the coldest weather they had ever experienced, and open hostility and racism. With this in mind, I find there's something quite sad and poignant about this song, with its hopeful attitude in the face of difficult times ahead.

So even though black people have existed in Britain since long before 1948, this song is a good place to start our journey, because the *Windrush*'s arrival marks the start of modern black Britain. And like the song says, London really was the place to be. Right up until today, the majority of black people in the UK live in London, which makes it an important part of the black British story.

However, as we shall see, the songs and sounds that help tell the story of black people in Britain travel very far and very wide.

'LET'S HAVE ANOTHER PARTY'

Winifred Atwell (1954)

Probably not the kind of song you were expecting in a book about modern black music, right?

Here's what you can hear . . .

There are the plinkety-plonks of some fast-moving piano playing. It's cheerful and happy, and you can imagine people laughing along while listening to it. And if you think it sounds like music from the old days, well done, you are absolutely right. It's a type of music called ragtime and it's from the 1950s, when ragtime was very popular in the UK – just before rock and roll came over from America.

Now here's what you *can't* hear . . .

You can't hear anyone singing along, or any voices at all.

This is because 'Let's Have Another Party' is an instrumental. It's from a time when lots of popular music didn't include vocals at all.

Another thing you can't hear is that the fingers playing all that ragtime piano belong to someone called Winifred Atwell. You also can't hear that Winifred Atwell is a woman and black, originally from the Caribbean island of Trinidad (just like Lord Kitchener and someone called Mighty Terror, who we shall meet later). I think what you *can* hear is that Winifred Atwell was very, very good at playing the piano.

Winifred Atwell was the first ever black artist in the UK to sell a million records. A million records. In 1954, 'Let's Have Another Party' also became the first piece of instrumental piano music to reach number one in the music charts. Atwell became so famous that the first ever black women's hairdressers in the country (probably) was named after her. She was even asked to play for Queen Elizabeth II at a private party. And at one point, her piano-playing hands were thought to be so valuable that she was actually legally not allowed to do the washing up, in case she damaged them.

This is all the more extraordinary because of what was going on around her.

One of the effects of the Second World War was that extraordinary numbers of people moved all over the world, fighting in different countries. Britain called upon soldiers from its various colonies, including India, which provided more than 2.5 million, as well countries across Africa such as Gambia, Sierra Leone and the Gold Coast, which would later change its name to Ghana, where my parents are from. The war also meant the arrival in Britain of black and white military service people from the USA, a country of deep racial inequality, still living in the dark shadows of slavery.

With the mixing of black and white people came lots of racism. In 1943, a sergeant from Barbados called Arthur Walrond was attacked by two white American soldiers at a dance, because he asked a white woman to dance with him. Winifred Atwell made the kind of music that everyone probably would have been dancing to at that event, but that wasn't enough to erase the ugly power of racist attitudes.

After the Second World War finished and the soldiers returned home, organisations such as London Transport, British Rail and the National Health Service started to recruit heavily from the Caribbean, looking to the colonies to provide the workers they needed. And this put even more pressure on race relations, as the white people who didn't want to do the jobs resented these new arrivals who did.

So it's incredible that Winifred Atwell was such a superstar. She played to audiences of millions on television and radio, and travelled the world to perform live across the globe. I find it extraordinary that this was all happening at a time when it was still perfectly acceptable for black people to be treated unfairly or discriminated against because of the colour of their skin. It wouldn't be until 1965 that the Race Relations Act finally made this kind of racism illegal in the UK. While Winifred Atwell was dazzling Britain and the rest of the world with her music, black communities in the UK were suffering prejudice and racism every day, including violent physical attacks.

It wasn't all bad, though. In the 1950s, some efforts were being made to unite black and white communities – and music was the key. In 1955, in the borough of Lambeth in south London, a special dance was held precisely for this reason. Local residents, both black and white, were invited to the town hall to dance together in a display of racial unity. It's a building that I saw every day on my way to school when I was growing up, but I had no idea that it once held a huge party in the name of racial equality. The dance was intended to make a statement against something called a 'colour bar', which means a system where black people were not allowed to enjoy the same privileges as white people. The 'No Colour Bar' dance was a hugely important moment for race relations in the UK, and it moved to a musical soundtrack, showing the world that black people and white people could dance together and live in peace.

*

Towards the end of her career, Atwell settled down in Australia, a country that welcomed her as a celebrity. There she often spoke out against the poor treatment of the aboriginal community, dark-skinned people who suffered racism from the white majority.

We're very early on in our journey through history and music, but this song might already be the best example of how pure talent and pure joy can fly high above racism, shining a light through some truly dark times.

'No Carnival in Britain'

Mighty Terror (1954)

Remember Lord Kitchener? Remember his song about how excited he was to be coming to London in 1948? Well, in the early 1950s lots of people were feeling optimistic like this. The war was over. People all over the world were rebuilding society and seeking new opportunities.

One of these people was Fitzgerald Henry, a man from Trinidad travelling to London for the first time in 1953. When he arrived, the first thing he did was jump in a cab and ask to be taken to Lord Kitchener. Which is a bit like if you grew up in the same town as Justin Bieber and heard he'd moved away and become famous, so you took a flight to his new location and asked a taxi driver to take you to see him.

Like a lot of new arrivals from the Caribbean, Fitzgerald

Henry was excited and enthusiastic about life in Britain. He quickly became a working musician, playing traditional calypso music under the name Mighty Terror – just like Lord Kitchener, he had chosen a stage name. But after three years of working and living in Britain, he wasn't making happy songs about London being the place for him. He was working on a much sadder song called 'No Carnival in Britain'. Which brings us neatly to this chapter.

Throughout the 1950s a growing number of people arriving from the West Indies faced hostility and racism. There were even new racist organisations being formed in the UK, such as the White Defence League, whose members believed that white British people were somehow under threat from the new black minority. They were wrong, but their beliefs were dangerous, and led to innocent black people being attacked.

In the summer of 1958, things boiled over. Notting Hill was a part of London that was home to a community of black immigrants (people who had come to the UK from other countries). It was in August that a gang of white men decided to go around the area attacking black residents. A few days later, a white woman was attacked after having an argument with her husband. He was black, which upset racist onlookers.

Then things got worse.

Later that same night, hundreds of white people gathered to attack local Caribbean homes. I can barely imagine how terrifying this must have been, to be targeted by a hate-filled majority – and in a country that had invited you in, a country you believed to be your home.

These attacks continued for two whole weeks. They would come to be known as riots. Black people tried to protect themselves and some fought back, but most of the people arrested by the police were white.

After 1958, Notting Hill needed healing. Beyond that, the black British community needed healing. Black people had just been victimised and attacked at a time when even some politicians were busy spouting racist ideas to the nation. In this climate of anger and hate, black Britain, white Britain, all of Britain, needed *love*.

A woman called Claudia Jones had the answer. Like Lord Kitchener and Mighty Terror, Jones was born in Trinidad. She then lived in the US before coming to live and work in the UK. She was a campaigner, writer and political activist, which ultimately meant that she looked for real solutions to social problems. In 1958, she started up a newspaper called the *West Indian Gazette and Afro-Caribbean News*, the first of its kind for black people in Britain.

Claudia Jones could see how bad things were for black people and how something needed to be done to boost morale and celebrate the good things in life. Her next idea was simple: to organise a black community event, a party, a celebration of music and dance to remind Caribbean immigrants of their lives in the sun.

The Caribbean Carnival was first held indoors in January 1959. By 1966 it was established as a yearly festival known as the Notting Hill Fayre. Then along came Leslie Palmer, a young ex-teacher, who had the vision to transform it into a much bigger event in the 1970s, inviting live bands and big sound systems, and making the parade route longer. As a result of Palmer's efforts, attendance went up from thousands to *tens* of thousands in just a few short years. It became the biggest street party in Europe.

The Notting Hill Carnival is a dazzling example of joy and optimism in the black British community, a huge annual event with pulsing parades, giant sound systems, colourful costumes, food, drink and live music, inviting absolutely anyone to celebrate West Indian culture in the streets of London. It's an explosion of colour and culture, blending a rainbow of black musical styles.

The carnival that Fitzgerald 'Mighty Terror' Henry was missing so much in 1954 has now become a permanent part of British culture, where you can still hear the kind of calypso that he helped bring to this country. Now, the legacy of Trinidad and all the Caribbean islands lives on and lives strong, even if there was pain and struggle along the way.

'Sweets for my Sweet'

The Searchers (1963)

So far, everyone featured in this book has been black, as you might expect in a book called *Musical Truth*, all about black British history. Well, the Searchers were a band from Liverpool, in England, consisting of four members, and none of them were black. Let me explain.

In the early 1960s, something interesting happened in the development of popular music. Black musicians in the USA had been busy creating genres that would change the face of American music forever – rhythm and blues (also known as R&B), soul, and rock and roll. These genres were powerful and raw and full of emotion, drawing their energy from the sometimes painful experiences of black Americans who had suffered racism and who were descended from ancestors who had quite recently been slaves. The blues in particular is a musical genre that can be traced back to slave songs from the American Deep South. By the middle of the twentieth century, black history was already a huge part of American culture.

Meanwhile, American music was becoming very popular in the UK. The growth of vinyl records as a way of listening to music meant that people across the UK could access and share the latest American sounds. Young people could go out, buy a 'record' on vinyl, put it on their record player at home and dance happily. And then, if they liked what they heard, they often copied it.

The result was the British Invasion. Don't worry, it wasn't anything to do with war – it was the sudden explosion of British rock and roll or R&B bands not only in Britain, but in America as well. Famous bands of the British Invasion include the Beatles and the Rolling Stones (who went on to become some of the most successful artists of all time). These were both white British bands who made black American music. The Searchers were another example.

In 1963, the Searchers had a chart hit with the song 'Sweets for My Sweet', which spent two weeks at number one in August. Plot twist: it was not originally a Searchers song. 'Sweets for My Sweet' was recorded in 1961 by a black American band called the Drifters. The Searchers' version was what is known as a cover version.

Why is any of this important?

First of all, it shows us that in the 1960s, blackness and black culture were entering Britain from multiple angles. You had calypso coming directly from the Caribbean islands, brought over by recent immigrants after the war. These West Indians were also bringing sounds like reggae into the UK mix, which would grow hugely in popularity as the years rolled on. Then you had black American music coming over the airwaves and being shared through hot new R&B records.

Secondly, it shows us that young British people were open to black music, even if it was most popular when being played by white musicians. Add it all up and you can see that there was beginning to be a little bit of black in the Union Jack.

But it was not as simple as that, because racism was still a major problem across the country. In 1962, the Commonwealth Immigrants Act limited the number of immigrants coming into the UK. (The Commonwealth was the new international alliance of Britain and many of its former colonies.) A few years later in 1968, it was announced that immigrants could only come and live in the UK if they had a father or grandfather who was born in Britain. It sent a clear message: people coming into the UK from abroad were not entirely welcome.

In the early 1960s, Bristol, in the south-west of England, already had a close-knit Caribbean community. As was the case in other parts of the UK where black people lived,

Bristol's West Indian community were the victims of racism. This took different forms – everything from poor pay and inadequate housing to physical attacks by white gangs. The early 1960s saw the introduction of race relations policies that were supposed to prevent some types of racial discrimination, but racism was still commonplace. This was a time when the black population in Britain was increasing dramatically, up from roughly 300,000 in 1961 to over one million by 1964. The increase in non-white faces led to tension and sometimes conflict across many parts of the country. Inspired by the Black Panther movement in the USA (a political activist group fighting for black rights), the British Black Panthers was eventually set up in 1968. It hoped to achieve better conditions and an end to discrimination for black people in Britain.

One of the forms of racist discrimination that made life hard for Bristol's black population was a colour bar on the local bus service. This meant that the Bristol Omnibus Company would not hire non-white people to work on its buses. You may have heard the famous story of the black American activist Rosa Parks, who was arrested after refusing to give up a seat in the 'whites only' section of a bus in 1955 in Montgomery, Alabama, in the USA. Her action led to a huge boycott – where people protested by refusing to use the bus service – and is thought to be a key moment in the American civil rights movement.

Back in Bristol, four young black men had a similar idea. Their names were Roy Hackett, Owen Henry, Audley Evans and Prince Brown. Together, they set up a group to try and fight racial discrimination, asking a young social worker called Paul Stephenson to be their spokesperson. In 1963, this group organised a bus boycott by Bristol's West Indian community, in order to make a strong point about the racism they were challenging. Other people, both black and white, joined in the boycott, and eventually the bus company agreed to end the colour bar and allow non-white workers to join bus crew teams. The Bristol bus boycott had been a success.

Two years later, in 1965, parliament passed a new Race Relations Act that made racial discrimination 'unlawful in public places'. This obviously wasn't the end of racism in the UK (if only it were that simple) but it showed the positive power of black resistance. (Much later, in 2009, Paul Stephenson was awarded the OBE, Order of the British Empire, in recognition of his efforts to fight racism and the impact his actions had on British history.) But even though racial discrimination was being challenged in law, racism was still happening.

This was a time when immigration was being limited and some politicians were encouraging people to be hostile towards new arrivals. In 1968, a leading politician called Enoch Powell made a speech in which he said that Britain 'must be mad' to be letting immigrants into the country. In the same speech, he warned that 'in fifteen or twenty years' time the black man will have the whip hand over the white man'. The speech became known as the 'Rivers of Blood' speech, because this is what Powell feared he would see in Britain's future. This was deliberately trying to scare white British people into thinking that they were losing power and control of their country, which was simply not true. These ideas were dangerous but popular, as we shall see as we go into the 1970s.

This might all be a bit confusing, but one thing is clear: black Britain was beginning to stand up to racial inequality and white Britain was starting to shift in its attitudes towards black people. In the 1960s, the fight for racial equality was very much alive in Britain, right alongside major changes in youth culture led by new black trends. While white artists were exporting their own remakes of black music back to the USA, black activists were drawing inspiration from American civil rights campaigners.

And all the while, the most popular bands in the charts were white musicians making their own versions of black American music. It sounds crazy, but it's entirely possible that those young, white Britons who were suspicious of black people were dancing away to black music at the very same time.

'Sweet Mother'

Prince Nico Mbarga (1976)

I couldn't *not* include this one. It's one of the most popular African songs of all time. I doubt if there's a single African person in the UK who hasn't heard it.

Growing up, 'Sweet Mother' was a song we all knew: my parents, my aunties and uncles, my siblings, my cousins, my extended family. It's one of the songs that helped bring black Africans living in the UK together. There's something so innocent about it. It's a song about loving your mother, which will be relevant for as long as people have mothers.

Prince Nico himself was born in Nigeria but that didn't stop his song from becoming a huge hit all over Africa. When it was released in 1976, Africans living in the UK were bonded together by their minority status. It didn't matter where in

Africa you were from; 'Sweet Mother' was – and is – a song that always sounds like home. That's why it's ended up in a book about black British history. It means something special to a lot of black British people.

Here's a fun fact: in 2007, thirty-one years after 'Sweet Mother' was made, the grime artist Skepta released his very own version of the song, all about how much he loves his mum. Skepta is about my age and has a Nigerian background. I can fully understand why he would choose to honour his mother in this way. It's no surprise that on his song he shouts out not only his mum but also his dad, siblings and grandparents. 'Sweet Mother' is that kind of song. It's a family affair, and a sweet little reminder of the global black family.

*

In many ways, Africa is like the mother of all civilisation. It's the second biggest of the seven continents (after Asia), and home to the first ever human beings in our species. And although we aren't all African, Africa is the mother to us all because it's the land from where we all descend. This is a fact that I think we can celebrate; it's something that brings us all together.

Millions of years after our earliest ancestors left the African continent to disperse across the globe, we now have a beautiful spectrum of cultures and hundreds of countries. Racism makes us feel divided and different, a never-ending argument about who is better than who based on where you live and what you look like.

Racism is not only dangerous, but it's stupid as well. You don't need a geography lesson for me to tell you the most obvious fact in this book: that we all come from one race, the human race. And it's a race that we can't win by hating each other over the colours of our skin. When you think about it like that, a song like 'Sweet Mother' becomes a heartfelt reminder that everyone comes from the same cradle, the sons and daughters of earth itself.

'Sonny's Lettah'

Linton Kwesi Johnson (1979)

First, let's take a closer look at what was happening in the 1970s. It was a decade in which my own parents arrived in the UK as economic migrants from Ghana, along with thousands of other Commonwealth Africans, with hopes of opportunity and prosperity. Brixton was already a hub for West Indian migrants and it was an obvious place for Africans to lay down their roots too, so my parents and aunts and uncles did just that. But it wasn't all rosy – as we will learn, courtesy of Linton Kwesi Johnson.

If you mute the music, 'Sonny's Lettah' is a poem, and it was initially written this way, to be read on the printed page. It's also a story. A story about a man called Sonny who is writing a letter to his mother from prison. The story goes like this:

- Sonny is out with his little brother Jim.
- Jim is waiting for a bus.
- A police van pulls up and out jump three angry police officers.
- Jim has done nothing wrong.
- The police officers proceed to attack him.

At this point, Sonny decides that he can't just stand there, so . . .

- He attacks the police officers.
- More police arrive.
- One police officer falls, is badly injured, and dies.
- Sonny is arrested and charged with murder.

'Sonny's Lettah' is not a happy song.

You can tell that Sonny is black because he sounds Jamaican, speaking in patois (pronounced 'pat-wah', a slang version of English spoken by West Indian people). If you read the lyrics, you'll see that Linton Kwesi Johnson has even written it phonetically, making you become a bit Jamaican when you read Sonny's words out loud.

If you were Jamaican, or any kind of black man in Britain in 1979, you definitely experienced racism. Black people had been discriminated against by white people on a daily basis, and were often refused jobs and housing in a country where signs saying 'no dogs, no blacks, no Irish' were commonplace. Meanwhile, speeches by leading politicians were helping to fuel racism, xenophobia and anti-immigration beliefs, such as Enoch Powell's 'Rivers of Blood' speech (mentioned earlier) in which he tried to scare the white British public into thinking that black people were taking over.

It wasn't just politicians and the general public from whom black people experienced racism. As a black man in 1979 you might have found yourself getting regularly stopped by the police. This was a time when young black men in particular were often suspected of being criminals without reason. This is known as 'racial profiling' and it still happens today. As recently as 2018, statistics show that black people are actually *nine and a half times* more likely to be stopped and searched by the police than white people.

Why? Well, tension between black communities and the police has been a very real problem since black people started arriving in Britain in large numbers, in the middle of the twentieth century. Black people have often found themselves to be the victims of prejudice and suspicion from the police, treated as more likely than other groups to commit crimes.

This is not to say that all police are racist. Instead we're seeing institutional or structural racism – where a whole organisation or system is biased against a minority group, sometimes without even realising it. Like a massive hurricane, or a nasty infection, or the amount of sugar in a bottle of fizzy drink, structural racism can do a *lot* of damage even though you can't actually see it. It can prevent black people from being hired into well-paid jobs. It can make interviewers think that black people are too different to fit in. It can make teachers be unfairly strict with black students. And it can make black people be seen as suspicious and dangerous by the police, when we have done nothing wrong. I was a teenager when I realised that I couldn't browse through shops without being followed by security guards who thought I might be trying to steal something. Even now, as an adult, I have a habit of always staying in plain sight when I'm looking through shop shelves, for fear of being approached as a criminal. Black people suffer these kinds of microaggressions all of the time, the victims of stereotyping that can come from all angles of society.

'Sonny's Lettah' is a song that zooms into a difficult relationship between black people and the police. The law that allowed the police to stop and arrest people without any evidence was known in black communities as the 'sus law'. Laws like this go as far back as the early 1800s, but it was ethnic minority groups in the 1970s and 1980s who suffered the most from their powers.

'Sonny's Lettah' is also known as the 'anti-sus poem'.

As a song, it is a piece of resistance against how the police were targeting black people. It's a song that makes you think hard about what it's like to be treated as a suspect and what happens when you fight back. The song doesn't pretend that physically fighting the police is a good idea (it's not!). Sonny ends up facing a murder charge and his violence doesn't actually solve anything. It's a tragic story, not an exciting one, with a slow reggae beat that makes you pause to think about how bad things are, rather than dance your troubles away. This is a song about suffering. Even the instruments sound like they're in pain, wailing in the background of Sonny's sad story.

And it accurately portrays life for black people in London in the late 1970s. Unemployment was rising and poor living conditions were standard. Add that to years of tension building up between the black community and the police, and you can tell that things aren't going to be pretty.

Music has a huge power to create change. Two years after 'Sonny's Lettah' was released, the sus law was repealed, meaning that police could no longer arrest people on suspicion alone. Many people believe that 'Sonny's Lettah' played a part in this, helping convince the government to rethink its attitude towards the black community. I find it incredible and brilliant to think that music had that effect. Listening to 'Sonny's Lettah' in the twenty-first century, decades after it was first recorded, I'm struck by how urgent and powerful it sounds. It's a song that speaks about oppression with purity and clarity. It's no surprise that Linton Kwesi Johnson was able to influence so many hearts and minds, having told such a simple, compelling and hypnotically rhythmical tale.

This could *almost* be a happy ending to this chapter, but unfortunately, the problems between the police and black British communities have not disappeared. Sadly, more than half of all male inmates in young offender institutions are black or minority ethnic, proving that black boys are still at higher risk of ending up on the wrong side of the criminal justice system. Meanwhile, the overall percentage of young black people in custody doubled between 2006 and 2018. I hate to break it to you, but this isn't the last time we'll see black boys falling victim to criminal justice in this book. At the moment, we're only in 1979, but we're already seeing trends that will continue to upset the black British community well into the millennium. And as we shall discover in the next chapter, these tensions could very easily boil over into major social unrest.

But you know what? The power of music to highlight these problems and spark positive change is the reason why I'm writing this book. The beauty of songs like this one is that they make us confront the ugly truths of prejudice and mistrust that black people have suffered in the UK. 'Sonny's Lettah' was one of the first songs to do this and remains one of the most important to this day. Better yet, it's only going to take us forty years and 132 pages until we meet young black stars who are influential enough to criticise politicians with the kind of confidence that was beaten out of Sonny's brother, confirming that right now things might actually be changing for the better. Keep reading.

'GHOST TOWN'

The Specials (1981)

Can you imagine living in an actual ghost town?

Stumbling through deserted streets, shivering at every wailing gust of wind, heart racing at every creak. Imagine the spooky old buildings and dusty, cracked windows, the abandoned shops and gloomy skies.

And can you imagine what would have to happen for the place where you live to end up like that, in real life? Some people don't have to imagine this. For them, it's just normality.

*

Urban decay has been a backdrop for black communities in the UK since black people started to arrive in this country in large numbers. It's what tends to happen to immigrants arriving in a new country: gathering together in large cities where there's a better chance of finding work and housing, but finding that the work is low-paid and the housing is run-down.

By 1981, this inner-city environment had become pretty normal for most black communities, and it came with problems. Unemployment had been on the increase since the mid-1960s. By 1980, 1.5 million people were out of work in the UK. For the working classes (people who have to work) this meant that life became more difficult. Shops were closing down, work was hard to find and money was scarce.

The song 'Ghost Town' is all about this environment. It's a haunting, eerie song that echoes through images of a very broken Britain. All of this should make 'Ghost Town' a depressing song to listen to, but it really isn't. The reason for this has a lot to do with something called Two Tone.

The Two Tone movement was all about black and white people coming together to make music and share culture. It was influenced heavily by ska, a traditional type of reggae music that young white musicians in places like Coventry grew up listening to in the 1960s. Two Tone took ska and combined it with modern genres to make a whole new sound that was West Indian, British, up-to-date and traditional all at the same time.

The Specials were one of the first big Two Tone bands. They were from Coventry but made music that sounded like it came from Jamaica. They helped bring ska music into the mainstream and had a bunch of top ten hits between 1979 and 1981. They had band members who were black and band members who were white, and they were most popular during some really rough times for Britain.

This was all really important in 1981. When 'Ghost Town' was released the UK was suffering from a series of riots in its major towns and cities. These riots were brought on by two problems: 1) the economic difficulties I talked about earlier, and 2) tensions between the police and minority communities, especially the black community.

Going back to Brixton for a second, 1981 was the year that the local police force's 'Operation Swamp 81' led to more than a thousand people being stopped in six days using the 'sus law'. The aim was to tackle Brixton's street crime, but in reality it made tensions boil over. Rumours of police brutality and an arrest were the final straw. Around five thousand people were involved in rioting, during which 279 police officers and forty-five members of the public were injured, dozens of vehicles were set on fire, and almost 150 buildings were damaged or burned.

1981 was also the year that a house fire in New Cross, London, killed thirteen young people aged between fourteen and twenty-two. They were at a party, and they were black. This was a major tragedy for London's black community. At the time, many people believed that the fire might have been started deliberately by racist groups. Tensions grew when the police failed to investigate further, leading many people to believe that the deaths were not being taken seriously. Two months after the fire, thousands of protesters marched through London demanding justice on what was called the Black People's Day of Action. They carried banners and marched all the way from New Cross to the Houses of Parliament – a distance of about five miles.

'Ghost Town' is special because it highlights how bad things were getting, while also celebrating black and white people coming together musically. In this way, it almost feels like a solution to the problems it is describing, delivered with Caribbean rhythms and a bit of patois.

In 1981, 'Ghost Town' spent three weeks at number one in the pop charts at the same time that riots were upsetting the country, proving that songs can be dark and moody but still shine a light of hope.

'PASS THE DUTCHIE'

Musical Youth (1982)

Birmingham is a large city in the West Midlands of England that is usually cold and wet. Jamaica is the largest Caribbean island, the home of reggae music, and is usually sunny and warm. If these two places were people, they would probably not follow each other on Instagram. But in 1982, they crossed paths in a major way.

Finally, we've reached the year I was born. (Happy birthday to me.) 1982 was a big year, and not just because I came screaming into this world. It was the year that the *Voice* newspaper was launched, Britain's first and only black newspaper, which is still in circulation today. It was also the year that 'Pass the Dutchie' was released by Musical Youth. But my musical history doesn't start with this song. I grew up hearing the songs we've already discussed, as well as highlife, Afrobeats, reggae, pop – all sorts. My sister was even named Marcia after one of the members of a disco pop group called Boney M. Music was always a huge part of my life and my family's life overall. To be honest, I think that music is influential in all of our lives, full stop. Just think about the year you were born, then google some of the songs you remember from when you were younger. I bet many of them are older than you. Our musical history pre-dates us.

A big way that any culture gets passed on from one generation to the next is through music. We can learn a lot about the world our parents grew up in from the music they listened to when they were young.

Because of this, young people are incredibly important when it comes to any culture's survival over time. If you don't teach children about culture, that culture will die, like a plant that isn't given water and sunlight.

'Pass the Dutchie' by Musical Youth is a great example of how culture can be led by young people. There's a big clue in the name: Musical Youth. Yep, a group of musicians who were young. Very young. Children, to be specific. In 1982, the oldest member of the group was fifteen, while the youngest was only eleven. In fact, all five of them were still at school in Birmingham when the group was first put together by one of their dads, a reggae musician.

62

The song itself is a seriously upbeat and cheerful reggae classic. It sounds like sunshine and fresh coconut water on the beach. It sounds like that feeling you get when you step off the plane in a warm country. It sounds like Jamaica because it is very Jamaican. It's part of a tradition of West Indian music being popular in the UK. It also sounds joyful and innocent, with those happy, young voices tinkling over those deep reggae grooves.

But back in 1982, no one really expected children to be recording proper reggae songs, which makes 'Pass the Dutchie' special. When the song starts, telling us that 'this generation rules the nation', it's an announcement that the kids are in charge. And in lots of ways, they're right. Throughout history, black British culture has often been led by young black people (something that we shall see much more of as this book develops).

But not only that, in Britain, black culture is a big part of youth culture in general. This means that black culture (including music, style and fashion) has always been popular among young people who aren't black. Remember – and I'll keep on saying this – black people represent only a *tiny* percentage of the UK population, at last count not much more than three per cent. So this level of creative influence is surprising and incredible.

'Pass the Dutchie' was a hit. It was so popular that it

reached number one in the UK pop music charts. Then it became number one in six other countries in Europe, number two in two others. Two things happened next:

1. The song reached number ten in the USA.
2. Musical Youth had a great time travelling around America meeting lots of famous people.

'Pass the Dutchie' was the fastest-selling British single of 1982, selling over a hundred thousand copies in one day. And this was before downloading and streaming, meaning that people had to get up, put on their coats and go out to a record shop to buy the song on vinyl. That's how popular it was. Now, this would have been a big deal for any recording artist or group, but it was an even bigger deal for five black kids from Birmingham, at a time when kids from Birmingham, let alone black kids, didn't usually become international superstars.

Birmingham is often referred to as the UK's 'second city', after the capital city, London. Birmingham is the UK's second largest city by population and has been home to black communities for many decades. Some of the most successful black British celebrities in British history have come from Birmingham. These include the comedian Lenny Henry, whose work as a humanitarian has helped raise many millions of pounds for good causes all over the world. Another famous

'Brummie' is the writer Benjamin Zephaniah, a Rastafarian poet and novelist who once called the part of Birmingham he grew up in 'the Jamaican capital of Europe'. (Rastafarianism is a Jamaican religious movement that started in the 1930s.)

In the world of music, Birmingham didn't only give us Musical Youth. It's a city with a long musical history, having produced an impressive list of famous musicians across a whole range of genres. Highlights include:

- The Singing Stewarts – a family of brothers and sisters who made some of the first gospel music Britain ever heard, back in the 1960s.
- Joan Armatrading – a hugely influential musician renowned for her unique lyrics and skilful guitar playing.
- Jaki Graham – an R&B recording artist from the 1980s.
- Ruby Turner – a soul singer who racked up eight hit UK singles throughout the 1980s.
- Jamelia – a pop and soul singer whose first album was released in 2000 (when she was still only a teenager).
- Laura Mvula – a gospel-influenced soul singer who rose to prominence in the 2010s.

You might have noticed how many women are featured in the list above. This, I feel, is a very good thing for this book and our musical journey so far. Birmingham has given us the power of black British youth and it has also given us the power of black female voices. When talking about an industry that is dominated by men (like so many other sections of society), it is important to highlight women and how much they have contributed to black British history.

*

'Pass the Dutchie' showed everyone that black British music played by black British kids could be popular enough to cause major waves all across the globe. In this way, it stands proud as a celebration of reggae, a celebration of youth and a celebration of black Britain, all at the same time.

And this is still happening. Right now, almost forty years since the song was released, we are seeing a whole generation of young black musicians becoming popular not only in Britain, but all over the world, with music that has roots in the Caribbean and Africa.

'Electric Avenue'

Eddy Grant (1983)

'Electric Avenue' isn't just the name of this song. It's also the name of a real place – a street in Brixton, south London.

Having grown up in Brixton, I know the street well. It's a bustling market, full of stalls selling everything from fruits and vegetables to clothes and handbags. Every Saturday morning, I would accompany my mum to Brixton market to do our weekly shop. I remember spending what felt like hours going up and down Electric Avenue and the surrounding streets, carrying thin plastic bags and taking in the sights, sounds and smells of a busy open-air marketplace.

'Electric' is a good name, because it always felt alive. When I was growing up, Brixton was still populated mainly by black communities and the market sold all the foods that African and Caribbean people would have eaten in countries far, far away. Yam, plantain, okra, garden eggs, oxtail, scotch bonnet peppers ... the kind of items you couldn't find in big supermarkets. It was busy, noisy, messy and full of life. Later in my childhood, I found out that Electric Avenue got its name by being one of the first market streets to be powered by electricity, making it an important piece of London history.

The song 'Electric Avenue' captures the vibrant spirit of this sparky environment. It's exciting and buzzes with a fizzy, crackling energy, full of pounding drums and crunchy synthesisers. But it's not a song about markets, food or electricity. Eddy Grant originally wrote the song in 1982, one year after the Brixton riots which followed protests over the 'sus law' and reports of police brutality against black people.

The riots had a big impact on Eddy Grant. His lyrics sound angry, but confident. He talks about being out in the streets in the dark side of town, calling on listeners to rock down to Electric Avenue. It sounds like a call to action, starting off by saying how the streets are full of violence and how there is work to be done.

He wasn't wrong. For years, black people in the UK had suffered from harsh social deprivation, with ongoing problems of poverty, unemployment and poor housing conditions. By the early 1980s, it felt like something had to be done to give black communities the living conditions they deserved and the fair treatment they had been denied.

The meaning of the song's chorus is open to debate. When Eddy Grant says that we'll take it higher, what does he actually mean? Is he saying that the people who rioted in Brixton increased tensions, taking things higher? Or maybe that protesting in the streets was one way of making changes happen, to rise high above social problems? Perhaps he was angry about the violence he saw in 1981, writing this song to highlight his frustrations about social unrest turning into fighting in the streets. The lyrics ask difficult questions about who is really to blame for social problems, alongside plain-speaking observations about a lack of food and a lack of money, meaning that people were hungry and unable to buy the things they saw on TV. He goes on to say that deep down, people might even feel like warriors, desperate to challenge society when they can't even feed their children or find space to hang out their washing.

Being interviewed in 2018, Eddy Grant explained that the song came with a sense of 'urgency'. He explained that the song was 'a wake-up call' for those who felt hopeless, knowing that when people lose hope, there is always potential for violence. These are wise words, a warning of how things can go wrong when people are pushed to extremes.

It's clear that 'Electric Avenue' is a response to difficult conditions that were being faced by black people at the time. In this sense, it feels like a positive moment in black British history rather than simply a song of anger. It has a positive energy that black British communities have maintained throughout the twentieth century and all the way up to the present day. If the technology existed and MP3 paper was a thing, I would make 'Electric Avenue' play out of this book when you first opened its pages. There's something about its restless energy and hard-to-answer questions that make it the perfect soundtrack for modern black history, and the empowerment that black communities have achieved out of troubled times.

'COCKNEY TRANSLATION'

Smiley Culture (1985)

Have you ever been told to speak properly? It might have been a teacher, or someone you live with, almost definitely someone older than you, right? Pulling you up and telling you off for using slang, or saying something that doesn't sound like what a newsreader would say. I bet you have, and when it happened, I bet you made a face like this ☹ (and then carried on breaking the rules anyway).

Breaking the rules of language is fun. It feels relaxed and, well, cool, because it's how real people speak when they're hanging out. For young people throughout history, slang is a major part of rebelling against adults who are trying to tell you what to do all the time, which is exactly why teenagers tend to use more slang than anyone else.

But it's not just kids who feel the need to not speak properly. Lots of people who don't have much power in society can use language to give themselves confidence and help establish their identity.

'Cockney Translation' is a song that does all of these things for black Caribbean people and people from east London, and it would get a double telling off for breaking the rules of how to speak properly in two different ways.

First up, patois is a way of speaking English developed by people who lived in the Caribbean. It is spoken in a heavy accent. You might have heard examples of patois, including things like:

- *Whag'wan?* (a greeting: 'What's going on?', 'Hello')
- *Ting* (meaning 'thing', as in 'Every little ting is gonna be alright')
- *Likkle* (meaning 'little')
- *Yout'* (meaning 'youth', as in young people)
- *Mash up* (meaning 'mashed up', or broken up, or run down)
- *Soon come* (meaning 'I will soon come back', 'See you later')

There are other examples but this book isn't a dictionary, so let's move on.

Next, we have cockney, which is a way of speaking English developed by people in east London. It's full of slang and phrases that take standard English and twist it around into something way more fun. As far as English goes, it is the exact opposite of what some people call 'proper' English, which is how someone like the Queen talks.

It also features something called rhyming slang, where words and their meanings are kind of hidden in other words that rhyme. For example: *stairs* becomes 'apples and pears', *face* becomes 'boat race' and the Queen becomes a 'baked bean'. Fun times.

Really and truly, there is no reason why patois and cockney would ever meet, east London and the Caribbean being so far away from each other. But when a generation of West Indian people came to live in London, it was only a matter of time.

'Cockney Translation' is a bit like a How To guide for how to understand both dialects, where Smiley Culture talks us through a long list of words and phrases from both sides. One of the first things that Smiley explains is that cockney is not actually a language, but rather 'a slang'. He goes on to explain that it is mainly used by conmen (people who trick you out of your money) and criminals. The idea here is that criminals can talk in secret languages that the police can't understand, allowing them to get away with even more bad stuff. There's a song from 2016 called 'Man', where the grime artist Skepta says he talks so much slang that the 'feds' can't even work out what he just said to a man. I'll let you work out if this is cool or irresponsible. Either way, it proves that there is still a link between street language and avoiding the law.

Even though patois is not a criminal slang language, black people who speak it have definitely been treated as outsiders. In the 1980s, black men in particular were viewed with suspicion. A lot of people held racist beliefs that black men were more likely to be criminals than other groups, which is simply not true. These beliefs are held by many to this day, even though black men and black boys are no more likely to commit crimes than people from any other ethnic group.

Not that I remember it or anything, but 'Cockney Translation' was released in 1985, back when I was three years old and struggling with the basics. Skip forward thirty-five years and the relationship between cockney and patois is stronger than ever. This is because of grime, the genre of music that originated from east London in the early 2000s. Grime borrows heavily from Jamaican culture while also coming from the home of the cockney. Grime artists often use patois in their lyrics, and many, such as Kano, Ghetts, Lethal B, Dizzee Rascal and D Double E (all from east London), also use cockney phrases.

There's no way that Smiley Culture could have predicted this, but the grandchildren of the Windrush generation (and many others whose parents came to the UK from African countries such as Ghana and Nigeria) have taken his ideas all the way into the twenty-first century.

Now, we can celebrate the fact that Smiley Culture was way ahead of his time, but in the end, his story is a sad one. In 2011 he was found dead at his home after a police raid. The cause of death was said to be a self-inflicted stab wound. This tragic event led to protests by people who thought that the police were responsible, arguing that he died when they should have been protecting him. In the song 'Police Officer' from 1984, Smiley Culture describes what it's like being stopped by the police when he's driving around London. These tensions with the police, for many black people, can lead to serious conflict. There's a history of black British people being victims of police aggression or police negligence.

Listen, sorry. I realise that we're a long way away from the happy place that this chapter started off in. But in a way, understanding that is an important part of the black British experience – the tension between outsider groups and the establishment. The fate of Smiley Culture is an extreme example of just how wrong this relationship can go.

*

In fact, here are a few more examples I think you should know about . . .

- 1985 – A thirty-seven-year-old woman called Cherry Groce is at home when the police burst in looking for her son. During the raid, Cherry is shot in the shoulder. She is left paralysed from the chest down.
- 1985 – A thirty-nine-year-old woman called Cynthia Jarrett is at home when the police burst in, searching for criminal evidence against her son, who was arrested a few hours earlier. He was later released without charge. Cynthia Jarrett has a heart attack during the search and dies shortly afterwards.
- 1993 – A forty-year-old Jamaican woman called Joy Gardner is restrained with handcuffs and adhesive tape when police raid her home due to suspicions over her immigration status. During the raid, Joy is unable to breathe and suffers brain damage. She dies four days later.
- 1998 – A thirty-seven-year-old former soldier in the British Army called Christopher Alder is punched at a nightclub. Christopher is arrested himself and is taken to a police station in the city of Hull. He is later found dead, face down on the floor. Years later, it is discovered that it was not actually Christopher's body that was buried in his grave, but the body of an unrelated black woman who had lived and died in the same city.

- 2008 – A forty-year-old man called Sean Rigg is suffering with mental health complications. He is taken into emergency police custody in Brixton, south London. He is left handcuffed in the caged section of a police vehicle and becomes unwell, losing full consciousness. He dies later that night.
- 2011 – A twenty-nine-year-old man called Mark Duggan is shot and killed by a member of London's Metropolitan Police who were trying to arrest him. Police reports state that Mark Duggan was armed. Questions surrounding his death lead to protests in Tottenham, London, where he was from. A peaceful march to Tottenham police station turns into conflict with the police, and soon becomes a riot. Unrest begins to flare up in other parts of London, and before long there are riots taking place in other cities of the UK, caused by a combination of protests against the police, simple copying and issues of poverty in the inner city. But it's important to be aware that these were not black riots – people who took part came from a full range of ethnic backgrounds. It's also important to remember that rioting can include senseless acts of vandalism as well as genuine anger and protest. None of this is easy to unpick. Society can be very messy.

- 2017 – Police in east London stop a vehicle in the early hours of a Saturday morning. A twenty-year-old man named Rashan Charles runs away from the vehicle and is chased and caught by police officers. He is restrained while putting an object in his mouth and later dies in hospital. The police are criticised for their handling of the arrest and their use of force. It is later ruled in court that Rashan's death was 'accidental'.

These cases are upsetting and difficult to even talk about, but it's important to remember them if we are going to really understand the struggles that black communities have suffered in this country. Figures show that black people make up around eight per cent of all deaths in police custody, despite being around three per cent of the overall population. This means that black people are more likely than other ethnic groups to die when being detained by the police. There are many possible reasons for this:

- Are black people treated with more physical aggression than others?
- Are police officers less careful about protecting black people who have been taken into custody?
- Are police officers expecting black people to be more violent, so treat them violently?

- Are there racist police officers who actually dislike black people?

There are no easy answers here but we need to keep asking the difficult questions. Otherwise, black victims of police brutality may never get the justice they deserve.

'BAD YOUNG BROTHER'

Derek B (1988)

I want you to imagine that the black population of the entire world is one big family.

Now imagine that you are in this family, and you are called black Britain. Your parents might be a country in Africa or the Caribbean. You have brothers or sisters in nearby countries in Europe, like France or Germany, where black people also live. When you grow up, your children will be black and British just like you.

In this way of looking at the world, black people across the globe often feel a strong sense of shared identity. In 1985, there was a big demonstration in London's Trafalgar Square where thousands of people came together to protest the system of racial segregation in South Africa known as apartheid. If you're black Britain, South Africa is one of your many, many African cousins, a country in which black citizens were suffering from racial oppression.

Meanwhile, black America is a bit like your bigger, older cousin. Black America is a bit taller than you, wears more expensive clothes than you, and even drives a car. Black America has been in America for a long time. It has fought for its place in the house and has even had its own president, voted in to look after the whole country. In 1985, the anti-apartheid protests in London were led by a black American activist called Jesse Jackson, famous for his long-standing work for black rights in the USA and beyond.

In the 1980s, black American culture had a huge impact upon black people in the UK. It might be hard to believe now, but many of the famous black people I saw on television, read about in magazines and listened to on the radio were American. This meant that black American (or 'African American') culture really shaped my identity as a young black person.

Derek B is a good example of this. He was a rapper who made hiphop music. In the 1980s, hiphop was fairly new and it was a movement that had come directly from the black American experience, starting in New York in the 1970s.

Derek B was one of the first British people ever to make popular hiphop music, which is amazing when you think about how many rappers there are in Britain right now. The funny thing is, Derek B even *sounded* American. If you listen carefully to 'Bad Young Brother', you'll hear him putting on an American accent, even though he grew up in north-east London. It's easy to make fun of this now, but the musical truth is that 'Bad Young Brother' is an example of the UK and the USA coming closer together through black music. As we know now, hiphop would go on to spread all over the world (you can get hiphop in any language) but it wasn't until the 1980s that Britain started to produce its own rap stars.

In a way, black America gave black Britain something to look up to. It had big, successful superstars like Michael Jackson, Stevie Wonder and Diana Ross, as well as politicians and business leaders who seemed close to making big changes. Of course, black Britain had its own successes and a healthy tradition of African and Caribbean cultures, but America always seemed so shiny and powerful and confident. Being a young black kid, we *had* to take notice and we were ready to emulate, or copy, their success. When Derek B said we should put our money on him, he was right: look at how big UK rap is now.

'Bad Young Brother' was released in 1988. It was the first time a British rapper had a hit in the pop charts. One year earlier, in 1987, Britain had seen the first ever black politicians elected into parliament. Their names were Diane Abbott, Paul

Boateng and Bernie Grant. It's clear that the 1980s were a time of great change for black Britain. Derek B was part of a new soundtrack for this confident new era that was influenced by America, but also separate from it.

'Buffalo Stance'

Neneh Cherry (1988)

For many people, labels such as 'European' or 'African' or 'American' or even 'black British' are not good enough for describing who they are or where they come from. Humans move around a lot and labels like these suggest that people can come from one place and be one thing. That people can be pigeonholed. That their ethnicity is just one thing or another.

Not true. Many of us have a mixed heritage, meaning that we have parents from different places. If you go back far enough, it's fair to say that everyone has lots of different heritages and countries in their genetic makeup.

Blackness is often seen as one thing. A lot of people who are called black are actually a combination of many different ethnic backgrounds, just like a lot of people who are called white.

This makes labels such as 'black' and 'white' misleading and unhelpful. You might have heard of other labels such as 'mixed race' or 'dual heritage'. These are phrases generally used to describe people who have parents who are different colours.

The diversity of blackness is a beautiful thing. Africa alone contains fifty-four separate countries, full of hundreds of different tribes and communities, colours and cultures, tastes and traditions, languages and lifestyles. This is why colour labels are so bad at doing their job; they ignore the fact that people are way more complex than just the colour of their skin.

'Buffalo Stance' is a song that bubbles with diversity. It's a fantastic pop song that confidently combines rapping, singing and electronic dance music. It shows us how confident black culture had become. It's also a song that shows us how confident you can be about your own diversity. If you listen closely, there's a bit where Neneh Cherry flips between a very British cockney accent and a very American New York accent. I've always loved that part. I sang along to it as a child (even though I didn't know what a 'gigolo' was). There's something fun about switching up the accent and not caring about which identity is right.

Neneh Cherry was born in Sweden. Her mother, Moki Karlsson, was originally from Sweden and her biological father, Ahmadu Jah, was originally from Sierra Leone. He was a well-known drummer who specialised in traditional African drumming. Neneh grew up in the USA and moved to London as a teenager, where she spent time making punk music and playing records on illegal 'pirate' radio stations (we'll hear much more about these later). Her stepfather, Don Cherry, was a famous jazz musician. Neneh's style reflects all of these influences, something that she is happy to celebrate – and so can we. It's also important that in a playlist full of male artists (in a world that is, basically, unfairly controlled by men) we have songs from groundbreaking female artists. This is something else that we can celebrate: that black women were taking their place at the very front of new, popular music.

Multi-ethnicity is a big part of the black British experience. A lot of people who are described as 'black' are biracial or multi-racial. During the Second World War, it is believed that around two thousand mixed-race babies were born in the UK, the result of black American soldiers mixing with white British women. These children were called 'brown babies' and many people saw them as a problem. It was a terribly sad time. A lot of these babies were sent away from their mothers to live in children's homes, where conditions could be tough and racism was common. In many cases, these babies' fathers had returned to the USA after the war. Under American law at the time, black officers were not allowed to ask white women to marry them. Isn't that incredible?

Nowadays, around 2.2 per cent of the population of

England and Wales is described as 'mixed', which is far higher than in the 1940s. Thankfully, people who are mixed-race or biracial don't face the same kind of rejection that the 'brown babies' met with. As we can see with Neneh Cherry, having more than one heritage is something that we can celebrate, rather than hide away from.

Unfortunately, there are still tensions between white British society and people who are seen as mixed-race people. This was shown by what happened to Meghan Markle, the biracial American woman who joined the British royal family when she married Prince Harry in 2018. From that point on she faced criticism from some newspapers and people who weren't comfortable with having a non-white princess in the monarchy. On one occasion, a radio presenter tweeted a picture of a chimpanzee, comparing it to Meghan and Harry's newborn son, Archie. Do you see why that's a problem? I hope so.

In March 2020, Meghan and Harry decided to step down from their official duties as royals, even giving up their titles. For many people, this is evidence of the struggles they faced to be fully accepted in a very white monarchy as a modern, mixed-race family.

But let's get back to the music.

*

We're now very close to the 1990s, where we shall see black British culture really take hold on youth culture, mainly through new music. With 'Buffalo Stance' we can see how the energy and excitement of new black music was ready to explode out of the underground, at a time when the charts were dominated by pop, rock and more traditional types of black music like soul and reggae. 'Buffalo Stance' is a very jumpy and hyper addition to our black British playlist, but, as we shall find out in the next chapter, new black music of the late 1980s could also be way more chilled out.

'Back to Life
(However Do You Want Me)'

Soul II Soul (1989)

Sometimes – not always, but sometimes – you can throw everything into the recipe and it still comes out perfect.

'Back to Life' is a good example of this. It's got a bit of a reggae groove, but with a kind of hiphop drumbeat. The vocals are smooth and soulful, but it has electronic instruments, like a lot of 1980s dance music. It's funky and easy to dance to, like disco, but it's also got beautiful soaring strings that feel a bit classical. And it has the simple structure of a pop song you would expect to hear on the radio.

In 1989, black British youth culture was becoming confident enough to make up its own rules, and win. I remember looking out into the world in 1989 as an inquisitive seven-year-old. I remember seeing young black people who were older than me, but not quite adults like my parents, aunts and uncles. They fascinated me, with their colourful clothes, cool hair and little touches of African style, like bracelets, beads and African-print fabrics. They were something I hadn't seen before. I didn't have the words for it back then, but they were a new generation who were taking black British culture in a new direction.

Soul II Soul were right at the front of this revolution. They were cool, confident and experimental, showing a little boy from Brixton that Britain was something that black people could shape as well as be shaped by. I love the fact that this song features violins so prominently. Classical music is often associated with posh white people and many people wouldn't link it with black culture at all. This song is a smooth reminder that blackness can include a whole range of cultural styles.

The woman who sings on 'Back to Life', Caron Wheeler, said this about youth culture in the late 1980s:

'You can't distinguish between colour any more – it's just people.'

This is an optimistic vision for the future and definitely something to aim for – that racism will no longer exist and people will only see people, rather than the colour of their skin. However, for people who are not the victims of racism, it can be unhelpful to ignore racial differences. Recognising race is an important part of understanding that racism exists. This is a vital step towards achieving true equality. Think back to 1955, when the No Colour Bar dance took place in Lambeth, inviting newly arrived immigrants to dance together with white residents. This was the kind of racial unity that was unusual in the 1950s but would be much more common by the time Soul II Soul were gracing the charts with their modern soul sounds.

By 1989, racial divisions weren't disappearing but they were beginning to crack. Years of black music had done the important job of bringing black culture into the white mainstream, inviting everyone to dance to the same tune, just like when Two Tone bands brought reggae to many parts of the UK for the first time. Only two years before, in 1987, the UK had celebrated its first ever Black History Month. This is further evidence of the growing awareness of black history in Britain, while Black History Month continues to be celebrated every year.

The 1990s were an important time for black youth culture. There was a confidence that was starting to shine through, led by fashion, style and, of course, music. It felt like blackness was coming even further out of the shadows and into the light, inviting young people of all ages to enjoy the brilliance of black culture. So let this one play long and loud, and imagine people of all backgrounds dancing together. It's an image of racial harmony that we can still reach for.

'World in Motion'

New Order (1990)

If I asked you to make a list of the most famous black celebrities you can think of, I'm guessing that many of them would be sports stars.

Like music, sport has been an area in which black people have excelled over the years. If you flick through the sporting pages of British history, you will see a long list of heroes from many different sporting worlds, including athletics and, of course, football.

Football is a big deal. Even if you don't particularly like it (like me), you can't escape it. It's everywhere. Growing up, I remember Saturdays being dominated by news of who beat who in the football league and which team was on top. This hasn't really changed, only nowadays football clubs spend hundreds of millions of pounds on the best players.

Then, every four years, you get the biggest sporting event in the whole world, taking over everything for the whole summer. I'm talking about the World Cup.

1990 was a World Cup year. It was held in Italy and it was one of the first World Cups I can remember getting excited about, back when I was a whole eight years old. For the first time, I was fully aware of the excitement and the thrill of watching your team go into battle on an international stage, twenty-two men chasing a football for ninety minutes while millions of people screamed their support at home. Living in England meant that England was an easy choice for a team to follow, so I found myself cheering them on.

Something that I immediately noticed about the England national football team was that it had black players in it. This is no surprise, considering how successful some black footballers were when I was growing up. There were three in total in that team: Paul Parker, Des Walker and John Barnes.

John Barnes is one of the most famous black British footballers of all time. He was originally from Jamaica and played midfield for Liverpool FC. For many black kids, players like John Barnes were an inspiration, proof that black excellence was alive and well in the world of football.

But these players didn't always have it easy. In the 1980s, racism was a huge problem in football. Black players would face racist chants from fans when they played in matches and they were still too much of a minority to be able to force the footballing bosses to make any changes. It is even now the case that some black players have bananas thrown at them from the stands. This is a racist action, suggesting that black people are like monkeys, a deeply offensive and idiotic insult that has its roots in European racism against African people. There's a famous picture from 1988 of John Barnes kicking a banana away from him while playing for Liverpool. In years to come, he would become a campaigner against racism in football, a problem which still exists to this day.

In 1990, John Barnes was a central figure in England's World Cup campaign. He was playing for a country in which he had suffered racism while simply trying to do his job. The country was excited and hopeful that the England squad, including John Barnes, could win the greatest footballing prize of all time.

But I was far more interested in his rapping skills.

'World In Motion' is a song by a group called New Order that was created especially for the 1990 World Cup. It's an anthem for England supporters, with a chorus that you can chant along to as if you're shouting from the terraces. It's a song that tells you to sing proudly for England (ENG-ER-LAND!) and right near the end it's got a whole rap verse from, guess who? Yep: John Barnes himself.

For eight-year-old me, this was all terribly exciting. Rap

was still quite new and there wasn't even a lot of rap in the charts. To see a black footballing superstar rapping (quite well, sort of) in a real-life music video was genuinely thrilling. I felt proud to be black and British. I was already proud of my Ghanaian heritage and I had lots of role models in my family, but it was refreshing to see black stars in newspapers and on the television, celebrating black culture. Looking back, I can see now that it was a big moment for black culture too, more evidence of the fact that Britishness was allowing blackness in, a little bit. There's a line in the song where John Barnes describes himself as 'the England man'. In a country where black people had been rejected and treated as outsiders for decades, this was a powerful moment of racial inclusion.

'World in Motion' was a moment of unity for English football fans, and black people were invited to sing along too. It wasn't the end of racism, far from it, but for a whole generation of people it was probably one of the first times that they embraced black culture (even if it was just in the form of cheesy rap from a black midfielder).

'It's a Shame'

Monie Love (1990)

In the 1990s, I was growing up with two elder sisters. I'm the only boy in my family and my sisters are six and eight years older than me, which officially makes me the baby. As the 1990s dawned, I noticed a new kind of confidence in my sisters, and it wasn't just about growing up and getting older. I saw them dressing differently, getting jobs, holding parties for their friends, learning new skills, passing exams and getting qualifications that would one day lead to successful jobs and long-lasting careers.

They were becoming independent. For years, I had watched them doing what they were told, but now they seemed to be taking charge. They had responsibilities and plans, and they were leading the way.

The music they were listening to was like a soundtrack of this independence. I remember sneaking into their room to look through their record collection. It was full of all kinds of music, but one of the main things I noticed was how many black female artists they were listening to. American singers like Whitney Houston and Mary J. Blige, or rappers like Queen Latifah, Neneh Cherry and Salt 'n' Pepa. I didn't have the words for it back then, but these artists were great examples of black female *empowerment*. They were proud and confident, making music in a genre that was, at the time, dominated by men. Thinking back now, these women must have been incredible role models for young black women in the UK like my sisters.

And then there was Monie Love.

Monie Love was one of the first black British female rappers I ever heard. My sisters had a copy of her single 'It's a Shame' on seven-inch vinyl – a small record that had two songs on it, one on each side. On the front cover, there's a picture of Monie Love looking like … a young black woman from London. Which is exactly what she was. Unlike some female rappers nowadays, Monie Love wasn't trying to shock the world with outrageous outfits or anything like that. She just seemed to be herself, wearing a hoodie and a smile. But that didn't stop her from having all the confidence of a rap superstar, even at the age of twenty, which is how old she was when 'It's a Shame' was released.

I can only imagine what it was like for my sisters to hear a girl from London, like they were, rapping on hit records. When Monie Love starts the song by asking her sisters what the trouble is, it's like she's speaking directly to young black women like her. She goes on to explain how young women shouldn't have to put up with unfair treatment, a message which is as relevant today as it ever was. 'It's a Shame' is an empowering song that is direct and strong without being aggressive, riding on a smooth sample from a much older song from years before. Monie Love's rapping is fast and complicated, cartwheeling through the drumbeat with serious agility. Black women are often criticised as being angry or aggressive, which is an untrue and unfair stereotype. This song is an example of how black femininity can be confident without being angry.

One year before 'It's a Shame', Monie Love featured in a song called 'Ladies First' alongside Queen Latifah, one of the most famous rappers of all time. It's a song all about female empowerment, challenging sexism in society and the unfair ways in which women are treated. The song also had a video that was very Afrocentric, promoting positive images of African culture. If you look closely, the clothes that Queen Latifah and Monie Love wear in the video are African in style, showing the world that black African culture was something to be celebrated. In 'Ladies First', Queen Latifah also calls Monie Love her European 'partner', a reminder that black identity was becoming stronger between the UK and the USA. We'll see more of this in 2004 when we meet the British rapper Estelle, talking about what it was like to grow up in the 1980s.

Monie Love is an example of the new generation of black British role models who were emerging towards the end of the twentieth century. She drew her confidence from her skills as a rapper, her love of American hiphop and deeper roots of black culture.

Interlude

A moment of silence

Turn off the music for a second. I want you to do something for me.

I want you to stop reading, close your eyes and count to ten, in silence. Ready?

Go.

. . .

Ten silent seconds. That's how long it can take to take a life. On 22 April 1993, exactly one month after my eleventh birthday, that's how long it took a group of young men to murder a teenager who was waiting for a bus with his friend, one dark night in south-east London.

His name was Stephen Lawrence, he was eighteen years old, and he was murdered because he was black.

There is no song for this. I don't want any music to distract us from this dark reality. This was a murder born out of pure, cold racism – pure evil, from a group of youths who attacked Stephen because of the colour of his skin. They didn't know him. They saw him from across the street, crossed the road, called him a 'nigger' and stabbed him with knives until he bled to death.

The racist attacks of the 1950s, 60s, 70s and 80s might seem like ancient history to you, and even the 1990s might feel like a whole world away from where we are now, but the echoes of this crime continue to reverberate through British history.

Because they got away with it. After the murder, Stephen's killers were not brought to justice. In fact, it wasn't until 2012, a full nineteen years later, that two of them would finally be sentenced to prison for their crime. It took years for Stephen's family to fight the system. His parents, Doreen and Neville, were originally from Jamaica and had come to Britain in the 1960s. Stephen was their first child together. Britain was where they grew a family and made a home, one that was ripped apart by an unthinkable tragedy.

So why did it take so long for Stephen's killers to be found guilty?

In 1999, a huge government report found that London's Metropolitan Police Service had failed to do its job properly.

The report, known as the Macpherson Report (after the person who led it), accused the police of being 'institutionally racist'. This means that racist attitudes within the force itself led to the Lawrence family not being treated fairly or taken seriously enough. There were three main criticisms:

1. 'professional incompetence' (people in the police force not being good enough at their jobs);
2. 'institutional racism' (racist beliefs deep within the police force) and
3. 'a failure of leadership' (high-ranking police officers not doing enough to fix these problems).

Stephen's death was a tragedy that forced Britain to look hard at itself in the mirror and face many uncomfortable truths.

I've grown up with the legacy of Stephen Lawrence's murder. In 1993, I was a confused eleven-year-old wondering why anyone would kill an innocent person just because he had the same colour skin as me. I've grown up with years of newspaper headlines tracking his parents' fight for justice – their failed attempts and their never-ending faith. I've watched his mother, Doreen Lawrence, become a baroness in the House of Lords, meet prime ministers and be given doctorates from top universities as a campaigner for justice. In 1998, the award-winning black artist Chris Ofili painted a picture of her called *No Woman No Cry*, with tears each showing an image of her son. In 2011, a jazz band called Sons of Kemet recorded a song about her called 'Doreen Lawrence Is My Queen'. When I met her myself in 2018, she simply told me that she was 'tired'.

*

The case of Stephen Lawrence is a stain on British history. It's a reminder that racism can take many forms. It can be an unprovoked knife attack on the streets. It can be the police failing to catch the murderers. It can be an entire justice system failing to help a grieving family, for almost twenty years. It can be a memorial for the victim, laid in 1995, being vandalised over and over again. It can be the fact that this tragic story is not taught in schools, so that young people like you can really learn about the racism around you. It can be the fact that right now, only two of up to six men who killed Stephen are in prison.

So. In recognition of this tragedy, I dedicate this chapter to a moment of silence. In 2018 it was agreed that 22 April will be Stephen Lawrence Day, a day to remember what happened to him and everything we have learned from it.

'LITTLE BABY SWASTIKKKA'

Skunk Anansie (1994)

Black women are often supposed to fit into a very narrow selection of stereotypes. In the music industry, black female artists are often expected to be glamorous and sexy, with big hair and flashy outfits, strutting across the stage and screaming powerfully into the microphone.

That's another big stereotype: that black women are always powerful and aggressive, or even angry. This is very unfair. Many people assume that black women can't be sensitive, or are somehow more likely than other people to react with anger when they are annoyed. It is a racist and sexist idea to believe that black women are in any way angrier than anyone else, just because they are black and female.

Another commonly held belief is that black female singers

will always specialise in styles of music that first became popular in the USA, like R&B and powerful soul music with lots of vocal acrobatics and high notes. Even today, if you look at the most popular black female artists, many of them will be in this genre of music, or rappers.

The final big stereotype is that black women are somehow scary or intimidating. In the 1990s, one of the most famous black British female singers was Melanie B, one of the Spice Girls, and her nickname was actually 'Scary Spice'. She was the only black member of the band, and at the time, it seemed totally OK to identify her as the scary one. I can confirm that black women are not scary just because they are black. I know a lot of black women, and, like everyone else, they are only intimidating if they want to be.

Skunk Anansie is a band with a lead singer who is both black and a woman. Her name is Deborah Anne Dyer, but she is known by the nickname Skin. Skin breaks a lot of the stereotypes that I've just described. First, she doesn't have big hair. In fact, she has very short hair – she's almost bald. She doesn't specialise in soul music or R&B. Her band makes rock music, full of chunky guitars and crashing drums, with quiet bits and loud bits. Sometimes Skin sounds angry. That's one of the rules of heavy rock music. And if you happen to be scared of powerful, confident people, then you *might* say that she is intimidating. For me, a better word would be *impressive*.

In the 1990s, I was starting out at secondary school. We hadn't seen anyone like Skin in the pop charts before. She was totally new, with a look that didn't fit in with any of the stereotypes and a confidence that made you sit up straight. She is also gay and has described herself growing up as a 'painfully skinny tomboy'. It's clear that she knows what it feels like to not fit in, in a world that often asks us all to be as 'normal' as possible. (Is there any such thing as normal, and who gets to decide?) But rather than hiding away, Skin made everyone see her for who she really is. Black, gay, female, rocking out and proud. It wasn't until 2005 that the UK would see its first ever Black Pride event, a celebration for non-white lesbian, gay, bisexual, transgender and queer people. UK Black Pride was co-founded by a woman called Phyllis Akua Opoku-Gyimah, offering the black British LGBTQ community the chance to celebrate publicly. In an important sense, Skin, as a famous black, gay artist, just might be one of the biggest role models of a whole generation.

Skunk Anansie's biggest hit was a song called 'Weak', which everyone knew well. In the 1990s it was the kind of hit song that was all over the pop charts and people would sing along, even if they didn't usually like heavy rock music. But before 'Weak', Skunk Anansie's first single was a song called 'Little Baby Swastikkka'.

You can tell from the title that this is going to be an intense piece of music. In the last century the swastika was a symbol of Nazi Germany, a regime that is infamous for deep racism and cruelty against Jewish people. After the Second World War (which saw the end of the Nazi regime) the swastika was adopted by groups who held racist beliefs, and this still continues today. It's an ugly reminder that racism still exists.

You will have noticed that Skunk Anansie spelled swastika with three ks. This is a reference to the Ku Klux Klan, a racist group that believed in white supremacy – the idea that white people are better than anyone else and should be in charge of the whole world. The KKK was formed after the American Civil War in the nineteenth century and may have had as many as 8 million members at its peak in the 1920s. It is often thought to share beliefs with Nazi groups.

All of this means that 'Little Baby Swastikkka' is a very political song. It's an anti-racist song that asks how young people can end up holding racist ideas so early in their lives. The lyrics describe a situation where a child has drawn swastikas on the wall, followed by insulting images of black people, described in the song using the n-word. This is a deliberate reminder of how nasty racist ideas are. The lyrics, rightly so, are intended to shock you into thinking about how racism can start so young.

It's incredibly powerful for this particular song to be sung by a black gay woman at a time when few black female singers were making political rock songs like this. It's a reminder that the black experience is not limited to the stereotypes that we always see, and that blackness has the freedom to break the rules.

'RE-REWIND
(THE CROWD SAY BO SELECTA)'

Artful Dodger featuring
Craig David (1999)

Earlier in this book, you'll remember that I described black communities all over the world as being like one big family. This global black family would start with the parents, who would be from a country in Africa or the Caribbean. Then you would get the eldest child who grew up in the 1970s, experimenting with new ways of enjoying traditional black culture.

Then there might be a few visiting aunties or uncles along the way, bringing reminders of what life was like back home. Younger siblings would come next, born in Britain and heavily influenced by American culture and fashions. That might be your Derek Bs and Neneh Cherrys.

At some point, the younger members of the family start to grow up. You might have seen this happen in your own family already, when elder sisters and brothers start to become independent, getting jobs and money and driving licences and flashy clothes, and going on holidays with friends.

UK garage is a bit like this.

Now, if you didn't already know, UK garage has nothing to do with cars. It's a genre of fast-moving electronic dance music that became huge in the late 1990s. It's bouncy and cool, and became most popular in nightclubs. As a type of music, it feels older than teenage, but younger than a fully grown adult.

It also sounds expensive. Going out 'clubbing' was not a cheap hobby. You might need money to get into a club in the first place, not to mention buying drinks and having a cool outfit to wear.

UK garage has often been called 'urban music', which means that it is music that originally came from the city. In the UK, the majority of black communities can be found in cities, particularly London, so it's not surprising that a lot of modern black music has been labelled 'urban'. It also means that many of the problems attached to living in the city (especially crime and poverty) would become subjects talked about in urban music, as we shall see later.

All of this makes UK garage an important part of the history of British urban youth culture. 'Re-Rewind' is especially relevant because of its deeper links to Jamaican culture. In Britain, UK garage showed us that even the newest styles of urban black music could be popular outside of the underground.

In the song, you'll hear the singer, Craig David, talk about the crowd saying 'Bo!' to someone called the 'selector'. In Jamaican dancehall music, the selector is the person who chooses which records are going to be played during a party. 'Bo!' is an exclamation you might say when the selector is doing their job very well. For me, the use of this phrase in a UK garage song is a mark of respect for Jamaican culture, proof that Caribbean culture is deep within UK culture overall. The tradition of rewinding or restarting a record comes directly from the Caribbean and is still a big part of popular black music.

Here's a fun fact: in 2016, the grime artist Skepta had a big show at Alexandra Palace in London, during which he restarted some of his most popular songs. A newspaper review of the show said that he had been experiencing technical difficulties. They didn't realise that he was actually doing what he was supposed to. This is a classic case of cultural ignorance, whereby the people in charge don't know enough about cultures that aren't dominant in society and make silly mistakes as a result.

*

A really simple point that I think is worth making is that black music doesn't have to be made by black people. Artful Dodger might have the name of one character (from *Oliver Twist* by Charles Dickens) but it is actually two people: two white men called Mark Hill and Pete Devereux. This is not unusual. A lot of the most popular black music of all time was created in the 1950s and 1960s by white rock and roll stars like Elvis Presley, or the Beatles, the Rolling Stones and the Searchers, who I've mentioned before. White bands were making black music at a time when racism was still an open problem in the UK and the USA.

'Immigrant'

Sade (2000)

'Black power' is a phrase you might come across when you start learning about the history of racism. It refers to the idea of black communities rising up in strength against racist oppression. In the USA, the Civil Rights movement of the 1950s and 1960s was all about black Americans finding power at a time when they were suffering from terrible racism, even being murdered and hanged from trees.

Black power is about making a stand. It might make you think of black people being angry and aggressive, raising fists in the fight against racism. All over the world, communities have come together in this way. In the UK, one example from the world of popular music was something called Rock Against Racism in 1976, when musicians were invited to lead the fight against racism through live performances and carnivals. Black power has often come through the sounds and songs of black music.

But power doesn't always have to be tough. Strength isn't always aggressive. It isn't always about breaking things apart or being bigger than everything else. Power doesn't have to be loud. Power can be quiet. It can be a whisper, or even silent. Power can be still and calm. Strength can be beautiful. Strength can be powerfully beautiful.

Sade is a good example of this kind of power. She is one of the most successful black female singers in British history, the lead singer in a band that is also called Sade. She is quiet and mysterious, famous for making the kind of music that melts into your ears rather than slapping you around the face. She is calm and sophisticated, known for her poise and composure, very different to a lot of pop stars who always seem to be making noise and trying to get everyone's attention.

In all of this, Sade is an incredibly powerful icon in black British music.

'Immigrant' is a quietly powerful song about how difficult it can be to fit into a racist world if you come from somewhere else. It tells the story of Sade's father, a Nigerian man who suffered everyday racism when he moved to Europe. It includes lyrics about people refusing to touch his hand when exchanging money in shops and being turned away from 'every door'. 'Immigrant' is nowhere near Sade's most famous song but it stands out as an important piece of protest music. It features on an album called *Lovers Rock*, which also includes a song called 'Slave Song', asking for children to be taught more about racism in modern history.

So far in our *Musical Truth* playlist we've learned about records that sold in the tens of millions, made by immigrants and the descendants of immigrants in the UK. Like so many British citizens whose parents were not born in the UK, Sade is the product of modern immigration. Her name, Sade, pronounced *Shar-day*, is actually a shortened version of her Nigerian middle name, Folasade. This name is a reminder that African heritage runs strong through black British heritage, as we shall see in more detail as we go further into the twenty-first century.

Before we finish, just take a moment to consider the fact that Sade turned a name that many people might struggle to pronounce into a name that is famous all over the world. That's power.

*

It's important to say that the late twentieth century was a period when many female black British artists started to take the world of music by storm. Sade was a 'household name', which means she was known by ordinary people up and down the country. Another successful black female singer was

Shirley Bassey, originally from Wales. Unlike Sade, who was famously quiet and cool, Shirley Bassey became known for her big, loud, powerful singing voice. She often sang huge songs that blasted with confidence, helping her to become incredibly popular across the world. From the 1960s to the end of the 1970s, she recorded three songs for three different James Bond films, the only artist in history to do so.

Artists such as Shirley Bassey and Sade were in the background of my childhood when I was growing up. I didn't realise it at the time, but it was incredibly powerful to have examples of successful, strong, black women in mainstream music. Thankfully, we're used to seeing this now, but respect must be paid to the individuals who paved the way.

'21 Seconds'

So Solid Crew (2001)

OK, so here's the thing. Violence and crime? These things happen. They're problems that don't seem to go away. They exist wherever people exist, an ugly part of society that can be found in communities across the country, across the globe, throughout history.

The UK is no exception. Open a newspaper in any given decade and you'll see headlines about knife crime or gun crime or street gangs – things that scare people and make for exciting stories.

When these problems get bad, people often try to find someone or something to blame. Music is an easy target. This is dangerous because it is unfair, especially if a type of music just happens to be made by one group of people and this group then gets blamed for problems that they didn't create.

*

When you think of pirates, what comes to mind? Men with parrots on their shoulders? Wooden legs and hooks for hands? Sailing the seven seas, saying *arrrrrrr*?

In the world of popular music, there's a whole other type of pirate that has nothing to do with walking the plank and looking for buried treasure. It all started in the 1960s, when some broadcasters decided to set up radio stations on actual ships, off the coast of the UK. These 'pirate' radio stations gained a reputation for playing music that you couldn't hear anywhere else, and they didn't get in trouble because they weren't based on land.

In time, illegal radio stations operating without a licence became known as pirate radio stations. In the 1990s, there were hundreds of them all over the country, no longer offshore but more often based in high-rise tower blocks where they could broadcast a radio signal most easily. We'll see more from these radio pirates when we get to the song 'POW!' in 2004.

I first heard So Solid Crew on a pirate radio station. Delight FM, to be exact – a south London station that I tuned in to once a week to hear the latest in underground UK garage. I would huddle close to my radio and twiddle the receiver until it just about locked into Delight FM, then spend a few hours listening to DJs and MCs having a party on the airwaves. It was electric. These radio sets, as they were known, were like a cross between a concert and a house party, right next to you on the stereo. The music was fast and new and restless, just like a teenager is. And the MCs would be rapping in accents like my friends and I had, from London. Their lyrics were clever and fast, with intricate rhyming patterns that I would imitate. Sometimes I would record the radio shows onto cassette tape and play them back on my headphones on the way to school. So Solid Crew were part of the soundtrack to my adolescence.

But they were also, like so many young black men, treated like fearsome outlaws, even though they weren't actual pirates at all. Why?

Pirates go around in a crew.

- So did So Solid. They even had 'crew' in their name, which made some people think that they were a gang, rather than a group of friends and musicians.

Pirates are dangerous.

- So Solid Crew made music, and some of their music talked about their experiences of growing up in deprived parts of London: living in council flats, having no money, working in low-paid jobs to survive and doing (as So Solid Crew leader Mega Man puts it) 'silly things' in the streets. They were linked to some violent incidents that happened at events they attended, including a shooting outside a nightclub.

- One of their most famous members, Ashley Walters, spent time in prison for being found with a gun. As a result, it was easy for some newspapers and even politicians to say that groups like So Solid Crew were dangerous. After coming out of prison, Ashley Walters concentrated on his career as a musician and actor, starring in films and television, and inspiring others to do the same.

Pirates look for treasure.

- One thing we'll soon see is that So Solid Crew were incredibly successful, way more than anyone could have expected from a group making underground music. '21 Seconds' was their first ever single, and it went straight to number one.

Pirates are flamboyant.

- If you aren't sure what that word means, watch the video to '21 Seconds', clock their outfits and imagine wearing that stuff in public. Now you know what flamboyant means.

Pirates sail all over the world.

- Sort of. So Solid started off as a very local group, at first limited to the parts of London where their pirate radio sets could be heard. But once they became famous, their success travelled, gathering nationwide attention. By the time I was at university, you didn't have to tune in to a pirate radio station to hear So Solid Crew's music – there were on mainstream radio, award shows, and even the television.

For people living in deprived areas, the threat of crime can sometimes be very real. This is the reason that my parents never wanted me to come home too late after school or hang out in my estate after dark. Historically, people living in poorer parts of British cities have often been closer to crime than they would have liked, including some of the most violent types of criminal activity. In 1998, London's Metropolitan Police service set up a special unit dedicated to tackling gun violence in the city's black community, worried that young black people were too likely to get caught up in gun crime. The unit was called Operation Trident.

Originally, Trident was intended to help prevent the deaths of young black people (especially men) in London. However, it eventually changed its focus to look at gang crime in general, not just gun crime affecting black communities. In 2012, a woman called Claudia Webbe (one of the advisers who originally helped set up Operation Trident in the 1990s) became worried that losing the focus on gun crime in black areas could leave young people at risk of becoming victims of gun violence.

This is a complicated knot to unpick. On the one hand, songs that talk about things like gun violence are just a reflection of the harsh realities of life in deprived areas. On the other hand, these songs might be glorifying violence by making it seem exciting, when it is really a huge social problem that needs to be solved. On the *other* other hand (we have three hands now), music about crime might just be art, like films about criminals that people can watch on TV all over the world. Rap music is often criticised for making crime seem cool. This is one of the things that was said about the UK garage that So Solid Crew made. But for me, their music was exactly that – *music*. To be listened to, enjoyed and celebrated.

*

For all the controversy and accusations, So Solid Crew are a dazzling example of black British success. They showed the world that underground black music from poorer parts of the country could make it to the stars. They inspired a whole generation to dream big and turn these dreams into a glittering reality.

In many ways, So Solid Crew are like a 'rags to riches' story, overcoming poverty to achieve huge success. This is true of many of the artists featured in this book, and (outside of music) many black people in British history. In 2005, a report from the Trades Union Congress found that black and ethnic minority people are more likely to be unemployed than white people in the UK. It also found that non-white communities were two to three times more likely to have low incomes or suffer from poverty, as well as the highest rates of child poverty. This has been the reality for many black people living in the UK – a life of economic hardship and struggling to make ends meet.

'21 Seconds' is proof that your environment doesn't have to limit your potential. Like the black urban youth of the 1970s, 80s and 90s, So Solid Crew were part of a social group who were not trusted and were often seen as dangerous, despite being victims of problems and conditions in their community that they didn't create. To overcome this in the spectacular way that they did tells us everything we need to know about how black British culture can grow to incredible heights, from the ground up.

'IT TAKES MORE'

Ms Dynamite (2002)

In 2018, Niomi McLean-Daley had a big decision to make.

Niomi McLean-Daley is the real name of the singer and songwriter known as Ms Dynamite. In the early 2000s her music picked up a whole bunch of awards, including two Brit awards and three MOBO (Music of Black Origin) awards. She made music that combined hard UK garage with smooth R&B singing and lots of rapping, and she did it well.

She did it so well that in 2018, she was invited to accept an MBE from the Queen – the very same queen who asked Winifred Atwell for a special piano performance back in the 1950s. (MBE stands for Member of the British Empire – the same empire that started our journey off back on page eight.

It is an award given by the King or Queen to people who have made an important contribution to British society.)

But Ms Dynamite wasn't so sure about this MBE.

For a lot of people, the history of the British Empire is not something to be celebrated. The empire represents inequality and injustice, a reminder of a time when Britain bullied its way around the globe, taking control of other countries.

Writing in the *Guardian* newspaper in 2018, Ms Dynamite explained that her first reaction to being offered an MBE was 'no way'. Can you blame her? Her grandparents were part of the Windrush generation who came to Britain in the 1940s and 50s, and were met with open hostility and racism, as well as very cold weather.

Even worse, 2018 was the year when the scandal broke that a number of people from the Windrush generation had been wrongly imprisoned and denied healthcare, supposedly because they did not have certain legal rights, though they had arrived legally from former British colonies when they were children, and had lived and worked most (or all) of their lives in Britain. Some of them were even forced to leave the country altogether. These were British people being rejected by Britain.

*

'It Takes More' is a very smooth-sounding song with very hard-edged lyrics. It's a song where we hear Ms Dynamite throw criticism in all kinds of directions. Here's a list of people she criticises:

- People who show off all their money.
- People who buy diamonds from African countries with unethical diamond industries.
- People who are violent.
- People who don't have any self-respect.

The central message of the song is simple: that young people need to think higher and aspire to be more than what you see in music videos and magazines. She speaks especially to girls and young women, who she asks to be independent and self-confident.

As a Windrush grandchild who made it as far as being invited into Buckingham Palace to collect one of the nation's highest prizes, Ms Dynamite definitely reached serious heights of success. The problem is that being accepted by the system that once hurt your ancestors can feel like failure.

But, as she says in the song, it takes more than this to confuse someone like Ms Dynamite. Her final decision was to accept the MBE, in recognition of the struggles faced by her grandparents. In her *Guardian* article she even changed the meaning of MBE from Member of the British Empire to *My Beloved Elders*.

In 2002, I doubt if Ms Dynamite imagined that she would be offered an MBE at all, but her music was about the experiences of young people growing up in the shadows of the British Empire. For black people with elders from former British colonies, there will always be some tension with the country we call home. Ms Dynamite grew up through these tensions, with a white mother who taught her about black history. As a child she was sent to a Saturday school that specialised in black history. It's easy to see how, years later, through pop music, she would lead the way in giving the next generation positive messages about being black and British.

In a 2004 interview with the *Guardian*, she said, 'Even when I was MCing I was writing about being strong and a woman . . . My lyrics have always been about something.'

We're getting closer and closer to the present day. Soon, we'll see how Ms Dynamite created a blueprint for young black artists to express themselves creatively and make political statements at the same time.

'1980'

Estelle (2004)

If you ever wondered what it was like to grow up black and British in the 1980s and 1990s, all you have to do is close your eyes and listen to this song. It's brilliant. It's basically a great big list of everything that happened in the average black household.

If you took all the lyrics, took out the rhymes, wrote them down in boring long sentences and added a few comprehension questions, you'd have a pretty good history book about black people in the twentieth century. Here's a list of ten highlights of black childhood you will hear in the song '1980':

1. Living with aunties, uncles, cousins and grandparents.

2. Going to church. All the time.

3. Having meals for eighteen people at a time (see number 1).

4. Boiling water on the cooker to have a bath.

5. Dancing – a lot.

6. Going to visit 'back home', where your parents grew up – in Africa or the Caribbean.

7. Watching black American TV programmes.

8. Church. Again.

9. Doing hair all the time.

10. Even more church.

All of these are important pieces of the black British puzzle, which is what gives '1980' such warmth. It sounds like a love letter to growing up black in the UK, because, basically, it is.

Some of the things mentioned in '1980' are about the USA. Estelle talks about famous black Americans who you might not have even heard of, if you were born in the twenty-first century. One of the biggest references for me are Kid 'n Play: a black hiphop duo famous for their energetic dance moves, massive hair and a film from 1990 called *House Party*. I remember copying their dances with my cousins and endlessly rewinding scenes from the movie, rapping along and feeling about as cool as a kid from south London could feel in 1990.

Another big reference is to a TV series from the 1990s

called *The Fresh Prince of Bel-Air*, all about a wholesome black family in America. As well as giving the world Will Smith, *The Fresh Prince of Bel-Air* showed a lot of Americans that black people could be just as successful and affluent as white people. When it came to the UK, black British people felt a sense of pride that black people on mainstream telly could be so successful and loveable at the same time.

It might seem unusual for a song about black Britain to be so full of American references, but there is a logical explanation. Black people in Britain have been such a small minority that there haven't always been a lot of us in popular entertainment, especially television and cinema. As a result, black British people looked towards America for examples of black culture in the mainstream, copying our American cousins. Growing up in the late twentieth century, it was totally normal for black British people to have black American heroes. We looked up to them and learned from them, giving black British culture a slightly American flavour, alongside African and Caribbean influences.

Fashion is a good example of this. If you look closely at the way black British teenagers have been dressing since the late 1970s, you will notice a lot of trends inspired by hiphop, which is an Afro-American culture. Baseball caps, sportswear, baggy jeans, expensive trainers, tracksuits – it all comes from the USA.

Right from the start of the song, Estelle lets us know that she was born in 1980. 1980 was the beginning of a turbulent decade for many black communities in the UK. It was a decade that will be remembered for riots and conflict in a number of British cities. In 1981 alone, there were uprisings in London, Liverpool, Birmingham and Manchester. A big reason for these protests was tension among people who had spent many years living in poor housing in crowded areas of cities, often unemployed or in low-paid jobs. A lot of these people were black. In the protests and riots that happened throughout the 1980s, race was a major factor. As well as suffering these poor living conditions and a lack of work, black communities had also been the victims of racism and unfair suspicion from the police. Their protests could quickly turn into anger.

In these circumstances, it's hard to believe that '1980' is such a positive song. It tells the story of growing up in a house of nine children and who knows how many adults, making £50 last for three months solid, with uncles and brothers going in and out of prison all the time. It's not easy growing up in poverty, in a situation where opportunities are slim, but '1980' doesn't focus on just that. It celebrates the good things about having a strong family in a strong community, something that black British people have relied upon since the very beginning.

'POW! (Forward)'

Lethal Bizzle (2004)

Question: What is *grime*? Answer: Grime is dirt. Grime is from the gutter. Grime is the filth you can't get rid of. It's not the kindest name to give to someone. If someone called you 'grime', you'd be right to feel insulted.

But 'grime' is exactly the name that was given to a genre of music created by young people living in east London in the early 2000s.

Grime music is fast. It's angry and aggressive, full of spiky electronic noises and cluttered drums, backed by growling basslines. It's exciting and energetic.

It's also very successful. Grime started in the streets and high-rise tower blocks of east London. It was created by the kids who weren't old enough to go out raving to UK garage, kids who grew up in a part of London that was suffering from economic deprivation. They took UK garage, mixed it with other types of music and turned it into something explosive and new. They went on pirate radio stations and laced grimy instrumentals with an endless stream of lyrics (or 'bars'). They talked about what it was like to grow up around poverty and crime, in communities that are overlooked by the government, turning frustration and energy into a sound that no one had ever heard before.

It didn't take long for grime to produce some of the biggest stars in urban music history. By 2003, artists such Dizzee Rascal were starting to create award-winning albums, and future superstars in the making were laying the foundations by recording underground hits and becoming famous on the internet – something that hadn't happened before. Grime might have started in the gutter, but it was always G.R.I.M.E.: Gutter Rich, In My Evaluation.

'POW!' is a song that fully captures the adolescent energy of grime. You can even see it in the name, which has an exclamation mark, like a superhero punching a hole through a building. It's so volatile that it was actually banned from some nightclubs, for fear of encouraging people to break out into fights. It's a song you can scream along to. In fact, the rapper, called Napper, has a verse in the song that starts with a prolonged scream, repeated a few lines later just in case you missed it the first time.

In the 2000s young people in the UK had something to scream about. In 2003, the government announced plans to allow universities to charge students up to £3,000 a year. This became law in England and Wales in 2006. Then, in 2010, the government decided to allow universities to increase tuition fees to up to £9,000 per year, meaning that many families would struggle to afford to send their children to university.

Large groups of young people took to the streets in protest. At one point some of them set up loud sound systems at Parliament Square in London and played music while chanting and cheering against the government. This is when the true power of 'POW!' was fully revealed. It was one of the loudest songs that got played, almost like an anthem for the protest. One journalist who spent seven hours being blocked in by the police during the protest said that 'POW!' was reloaded three times in a row.

The point here isn't that violent confrontation with the police is ever a good idea. The point is that here we have a generation of young people who felt that they didn't have control over their future and wanted to show their anger. 'POW!' captures this spirit. Speaking to a newspaper in 2011, Lethal Bizzle asked a simple but serious question: if musicians can make music that goes up against the police in massive political protests, then 'who's really got the power?'

He also called the prime minister at the time, David Cameron, 'a donut'. This is not the first time that a musician has insulted a politician. It will happen again twice before this book is finished.

Just like we saw with the Specials in 1981 and we shall see again with Stormzy and Dave in 2019, black music, political anger and youth culture are a powerful combination. In 2010, 'POW!' provided the right kind of energy for young people in London to express their frustrations with the government. You won't find a song like 'POW!' in a normal history book, but it definitely stands tall as part of the protest soundtrack of modern times.

'Black Boys'

Bashy (2009)

A stereotype is a tricky thing to explain, but I'll have a go.

A stereotype is when a group of people are all thought to act in a certain way or have the same characteristics, even if they don't. This is dangerous because it affects the way people treat certain groups as well as what they think of them.

Young people are often stereotyped. If you've ever been out with some friends and adults have started giving you wary looks before you've even done anything, that might be because they have stereotypical ideas about groups of kids getting up to no good. Being treated differently because of a negative stereotype is an example of prejudice (judging someone before they have acted).

Black boys are one stereotyped group who end up suffering

from prejudice that they can't control. It has a lot to do with 'unconscious bias'.

Unconscious bias is a very dangerous kind of prejudice that makes people treat different groups of people in different ways without necessarily realising it. It can be found in all kinds of institutions, including schools. In the world of education, the damage can be done very quickly indeed. Let me explain.

True: In the year up to 2017, the number of black students who were permanently excluded from school in the UK was almost three times higher than the next highest ethnic group.

True: In the same time period, the number of excluded Caribbean students was double the number of black students overall, meaning that way more black Caribbean boys get kicked out of school than black African boys.

Very untrue: The idea that black students are naturally more troublesome than other ethnic groups.

Very untrue and very dangerous: The idea that black boys are more likely to be disruptive and fail at their studies. This idea is deeply racist.

There are a few difficult questions we need to ask before we get to the song, and I should explain that the relationship between black boys and formal education has been a notoriously difficult one for many generations. Year after year, black boys underperform in national exams compared to other groups. Many are pushed out or excluded from school before they even get the chance to sit the exams.

Understanding why this happens is a bit like asking what came first, the chicken or the egg? Are black boys less likely to co-operate with schools and teachers because of how they are treated? Or are they treated unfairly because they choose not to co-operate in the first place?

Whatever the case, research has shown that the education system is biased against black achievement. This includes:

- Teachers having lower expectations of black students.
- Teachers expecting black students to misbehave.
- Schools being harder on discipline with black boys, because they expect them to be disruptive in the first place.

'Black Boys' is a song that actually celebrates black boys. It's a glowing love letter, cheering for every black boy who has grown up into a successful black man.

For the black British community, a song like this is a big deal. Bashy makes it very clear that he supports black success, which often has to fight against a system that doesn't want it or expect it. That's why he spends most of the song listing examples of black boys who have done well in the world, not hooligans, but young and talented Nubians. (Nubians are a group of people from sub-Saharan Africa. They are thought to be one of the earliest civilisations in human history, living in what has been called 'the cradle of civilisation'.)

Not that I've counted or anything, but in the space of four minutes and five seconds Bashy manages to shout out over a hundred black men and women in a range of professions including sport, entertainment, business and politics. It's an impressive list of people who have had a massive impact on not only black British history, but British history overall, a reminder that black kids grow up into black adults whose achievements are more important than the way they were treated in the past.

For me, the most powerful line of the song is the one where Bashy reminds us that it can be done: that black kids, black boys especially, can find success in a world that often holds us back. If you were starting to feel that this book was a bit dark, or starting to lose hope, or maybe a bit depressing in places, first, welcome to being black in modern Britain. Second, let 'Black Boys' shine a beam of hope straight out of these pages and into the future, which is exactly what Bashy intended for it to do.

'AZONTO'

Fuse ODG (2012)

'Afro-Caribbean' is a bit of a deceptive label for black people in the UK. It suggests that the African and Caribbean communities have had equal levels of influence on black British identity over recent decades.

This is simply not true.

Just look at the playlist of songs in this book so far. So many of them are Caribbean in origin, proving that black British culture has for a long time been associated with West Indian culture.

A lot of people won't know this but there's a bit of sibling rivalry between Africa and the Caribbean. When I was growing up, the cool version of being black was Jamaican. You couldn't escape it: the music, the style, the slow walk (what we called a 'bop'), the patois, the slang – all of it came straight from Jamaican culture. This meant that for kids of African descent, like me, it was a struggle to get out of the shadows of Jamaican cool.

The grime artist Skepta has a verse on a song called 'Ojuelegba' where he explains that when he was growing up, being African was a 'diss' (an insult) and teachers needed help pronouncing his name. Skepta's real name is Joseph Adenuga. Like a lot of African boys of that generation, he was wary of pronouncing his Nigerian surname for fear of being picked on by his classmates.

For most of my life, Jamaican culture was the cool part of black British culture. This didn't really change until 2012, when something called the Azonto hit the mainstream.

Azonto is two things:

1. It's the name of a song.
2. It's the name of a dance.

In 2012, it also became a phenomenon in black music, introducing a new Afrobeats dance craze to dancefloors all over the world, all the way from Ghana, west Africa.

It's a very happy song, with an exuberant dance to match. The song bubbles along on a sunny, bouncy rhythm. It's also a dance that you can customise by miming any action you want while you do it. Washing the dishes . . . driving a car . . . anything, really. There's something very fun and very African about this. It's a bit of a stereotype, yes, that black people love to dance, but at the same time . . . well, a lot of black people really do love to dance. Dancing is a big part of African culture and Africa is a continent full of traditional dances. But the Azonto was the first to have an impact on mainstream culture, bringing a new wave of Afrobeats into the new millennium.

Nowadays, it's not unusual to see and hear African rhythms, sounds and accents in popular black music. Afrobeats and Afroswing have taken off in a big way, with artists like Burna Boy, J Hus and Wizkid featuring heavily in urban music playlists. As Fuse ODG says in the lyrics to the song, it's time for the whole world to see what African culture can do. Born in the UK, Fuse grew up in Ghana and, like a lot of British Africans, he can call both places home.

The most refreshing thing about 'Azonto' is that it isn't serious. It's a party song that toddlers can bounce around to while grandparents clap in the background. Even though the lyrics talk about rising up against haters who want to see you in a crisis, it's not moody or dark or painful. It shows us that popular black music in the twenty-first century doesn't have to be cool to be cool, which, I think, is very cool.

*

People think about Africa in lots of different ways. One way is as the 'cradle of civilisation', like I did back on page 168. This highlights the importance of Africa as the place on our planet where all people originally came from, many millions of years ago.

Another way people think about Africa is as a dark, scary place full of jungles and terrifying animals that will eat you up. In fact, Africa was once labelled 'the dark continent' by European explorers (even though the sun shines quite a lot in most African countries, except at night).

A third way that people think about Africa is as a place of great poverty and suffering. You may have heard some parts of the world, including Africa, being described as 'the third world'. This is an out-of-date label given to regions that were not economically powerful.

Many people who have never visited an African country believe that the whole continent is undeveloped and run down, without basic things like solid homes and electricity. This image has been partly created by newspapers and television. When I was growing up in the early 1980s, Ethiopia suffered a huge famine that killed hundreds of thousands of people and left many more hungry and destitute. For years, many people thought the horrible images of famine that were shown in the media were an example of what life was like all over Africa, despite the facts that:

a) Famines have occurred all over the world, throughout history.
b) Ethiopia, like every country in the world, has a complicated combination of wealth and poverty.

While it is true that some African countries have greater levels of poverty that other countries in the world, it is wrong to think that Africa as a whole is defined by poverty. In Africa you will also find huge mega-cities such as Luanda, the capital of Angola, Nairobi in Kenya, Cairo in Egypt and Dar es Salaam in Tanzania. These cities are full of skyscrapers and motorways, pioneering engineering and cutting-edge sustainable technologies. All of this alongside ancient traditions and historic communities, such as the ancient ruins of Aksum in Ethiopia, Nigeria's Kano (west Africa's oldest city) and the historic city of Abomey in Benin. These sites are like a portal to the past. Africa is a fascinating mix of the old and the new.

'Azonto' marks the birth of a new outlook on Africa for the twenty-first century. Africa has always been a place of innovation, creativity, success and power, but for many years, people in the 'first world' just believed it was some dark hole full of uneducated people living in mud huts. Now, we know better. In fact, another Fuse ODG song from 2014 is called 'This Is New Africa' for this very reason. It's all about the strength of modern Africa and the pride that Africans can have in their heritage. If children in Britain learned just a little bit more about the more positive sides of African history, then none of this would come as a surprise.

'Shape of You'

Ed Sheeran (2017)

Here's something you can work out from looking carefully at the picture opposite . . .

Ed Sheeran is not black.

You'll have noticed that Ed Sheeran is white. He is from England, a country that is mainly populated by white people. Around 82 per cent of people in England and Wales are white and British, and Ed Sheeran is one of them. He is also a very successful musician. A quick maths lesson will help.

2.4 billion = The number of times 'Shape of You' had been streamed on Spotify when I wrote this chapter, making it the most streamed song of all time. (Please note: 2.4 billion is a very, very, very, *very* large number.)

0.004 = The number of pence, roughly, that an artist earns each time one of their songs is streamed on Spotify. (Please note: 0.004 is a very, very, very, *very* small number.)

In numbers, 2.4 billion looks like this: 2,400,000,000

2,400,000,000 x 0.004 = 9,600,000

Fact: there are 100 pennies in a pound.

9,600,000 (pennies) ÷ 100 = 96,000 (pounds).

Fact: I'm no mathematician, but this means that Ed Sheeran has earned almost £100,000 from one song getting played on one music streaming service. That's how much of a hit 'Shape of You' is.

I have seven other equally important facts to share.

Seven Other Equally Important Facts

1. 'Shape of You' is a popular song.
2. Popular songs are also known as 'pop' songs.
3. Not all pop songs are popular.
4. Not all popular songs are pop.
5. 'Shape of You' has a dancehall rhythm.
6. Dancehall is a genre of music originating from Jamaica.
7. Ed Sheeran is not Jamaican.

For 'Shape of You' to be Ed Sheeran's most popular

song says a lot about the impact of Jamaican culture (and black music in general) on British society. It's Ed Sheeran's blackest-sounding song and even had a remix featuring the grime superstar Stormzy, who is one of the blackest celebrities in modern pop. The song's popularity tells us that British people (and other people all over the world) are fully ready for Caribbean sounds to dominate the pop charts. In the UK, the song was even used in adverts for Marks & Spencer, which is one of the most British companies in human history. It's taken us a while to get here, but we can safely say that black music is officially part of British society.

This might feel dangerously close to a *they all lived happily ever after* type of ending to this chapter, but as with most things to do with race, it's never going to be that simple.

A lot of people don't realise that 'Shape of You' is a dancehall song, which means they don't realise that it is black music. It doesn't matter that Ed Sheeran isn't black, because his music definitely is. He was even nominated for four Music of Black Origin (MOBO) awards between 2011 and 2014. But does black music get the same level of respect and recognition that he does? I'm not so sure. We've reached a place where black culture is clearly a huge part of the British culture, but blackness is still massively underrepresented in British society. The biggest star in black music is white, and English, which says a lot about how far we have to go.

So while it's easy to celebrate Ed Sheeran as an example of black culture taking root in British society, it's also frustrating that a black British pop star hasn't seen the same levels of success. Yet. The next chapter might change all of that, forever.

'Vossi Bop'

Stormzy (2019)

On 28 June 2019, a grime artist called Stormzy performed at a festival called Glastonbury, and it was an iconic moment in black British history. I've never been to Glastonbury. Unlike the Notting Hill Carnival, it's not free and it's pretty hard to get a ticket. And I gave my tent to a friend about ten years ago and haven't seen it since (true story). But, like millions of music fans, in 2019 I was watching it at home. I really wanted to see how one of the youngest artists to ever headline the Glastonbury main stage would handle the pressure.

It was the first time that a black solo British artist had headlined on the festival's main stage, putting grime and black culture directly in the spotlight. The build-up was intense. At this point, I should probably remind you that I have written more about Stormzy than any other professional, published writer that I can think of. Seriously, I've written articles for national newspapers about him, countless tweets on social media, and he was a major part of my first book about grime. So it was with more than a little curiosity that I sat back to see what Big Mike (that's one of Stormzy's nicknames) would do with his moment.

As a performance, it did much more than give us a selection of Stormzy's greatest hits. It was also a political statement. Now I know that 'political' might not be the most exciting word you've read in this book, and I understand if you are tempted to slam it shut and slide open your phone right now, but please, bear with me. Politics is a vitally important thing that affects us all.

Clearly, Stormzy isn't a politician. He doesn't wear a suit, he makes good music and you can't vote for him. But he does speak out on political issues that he thinks are important: who should run the country, who shouldn't run the country, who we should trust, who's getting too big for their boots . . . that sort of thing. By doing this, Stormzy has accidentally become one of the most influential British celebrities of this century.

Here's one example of just how influential he is. November 2019: Stormzy takes to social media to encourage people to register to vote ahead of the upcoming general election. After his posts? A 236 per cent increase in new voter registrations.

Over 350,000 people who decided to vote after Stormzy said it was a good idea. That's power.

'Vossi Bop' is not the most political song in the world, in this book, or even in Stormzy's own catalogue of music. It's a song that's mainly about being cool and knowing it, flying overseas, not wearing a chain, and meeting your girl at the coffee shop, not necessarily in that order. But in and among all the bragging Stormzy does something very political. He attacks the government and tells us exactly what he thinks of the prime minister, Boris Johnson. It's a wildly passionate moment of political activism, asking everyone listening to dismiss the government (using language that I can't repeat here or we'll all get in trouble).

In the video to 'Vossi Bop' (which dropped back in April 2019) there's a part where a group of people in blond Boris Johnson wigs all fall over in front of the Bank of England, while Stormzy tells us that rule number two is to not make promises you can't keep, because if you can't keep the deal, it's better to just be honest. At a time when politicians (even prime ministers) can lose the trust of so many people, this is a bold and important thing to say so aggressively and clearly.

It's a controversial way to criticise the people who run the country. But the fact that Stormzy is able to do this says a lot about how far the black British community has come since the days of empire rule. Let's not forget, Stormzy is a young black grime artist from a single-parent household in London, the son of immigrants from Ghana, a country that was controlled by Great Britain up until 1957. Stormzy is a child of modern Britain, one of the black boys Bashy was rapping about in 2009. When you think about it like that, it's amazing that someone like Stormzy has become as influential as he has.

As well as setting records as a pop/grime star, Stormzy has also set up a scholarship helping black students to secure places at Cambridge University, a move that drew criticism from some people who thought he was being unfair to only offer this help to black students. This is obviously nonsense because the whole point of fighting discrimination is to target help at the people who need it most. As Stormzy says in the song 'Crown', setting up a black scholarship isn't anti-white; it's pro-black. There's a difference.

While we're on the topic, 'Crown' is a beautiful song. It's a quietly confident anthem about black pride that also tackles the pain of black struggle. It's a song where Stormzy searches every corner of his mind for answers that he can't find, which is a pretty good description of what it's like to be a victim of racial discrimination. But it's uplifting. Stormzy sings alongside a choir with a purity and honesty that reminds you of going to church, while a UK garage beat in the background reminds you of the history of modern black British music. It's calm like Sade but bouncy like So Solid Crew, with the smoothness of

Soul II Soul and the lyrical confidence of Bashy. The quiet piano and haunting vocals feel like wind in the night-time, full of tension and mystery. It's a celebration of black success in the face of adversity, which is one of the most poignant types of success you can get.

The bottom line is that Stormzy is important. There's a picture of him in the National Portrait Gallery in London, and people like me keep on writing about him in national newspapers. He's even put his weight behind achieving more diversity in UK publishing, setting up Merky Books, an imprint focusing on black writers.

Add it all up and two conclusions are clear:

1. Stormzy will absolutely go down in history as one of the most influential black celebrities of the twenty-first century.

It wasn't just the fireworks and kids on bikes doing wheelies that made Stormzy's Glastonbury performance so exciting. It was the interlude in which he talked about how black ballet dancers have been overlooked and forced to wear shoes that don't match their skin colour. It was the speech by black MP David Lammy, played to an audience of thousands in the middle of a (very white) music festival. It was the incredible shout out he gave to over sixty young black British artists making young black British music. It was the Union Jack stab vest he wore, designed by the notorious street artist Banksy, making a bold statement about rising knife violence in the UK. It was all of this, led by a child of black Britain with confidence and passion. That's why we're still talking about it. That's why it's important. And that's why conclusion number 2 is more true than ever:

2. Black Britain is continuing to change Britain, forever.

'Black'

Dave (2019)

So where do we go from here? This whole book has been about exploring black history and now here we are on the edge of 2020. Where do we go now? What does the future look like?

In 2019, a young rapper called Dave looked like the future, or at least part of a generation of young artists taking UK rap into the future.

Sometimes you have to look back before you go forward. The song 'Black' does exactly this. It explores what it means to be black and British in the twenty-first century by looking carefully at black history. It's a slow, thoughtful song that talks about what it was like for African and Caribbean people who came to live and work in the UK, the difficulties people faced with poverty and prejudice, and the strength we draw from our community. There is sadness in this song. Going further back, 'Black' talks about the history of colonialism that ripped Africa apart centuries ago, leaving place names like the Grain Coast, the Gold Coast, the Ivory Coast and the Slave Coast, based on what traders found most valuable.

But it also talks about how beautiful it is to be black. How black culture has been so popular for so many years, steering mainstream culture along the way.

Dave is young, only twenty years old when he wrote 'Black', but his words sound old and wise. In 2020, Dave performed a live version of 'Black' with extra lyrics criticising the government and calling the prime minister, Boris Johnson, racist. Later that year, during the COVID-19 lockdown, he posted messages on Instagram accusing the government of not caring about NHS workers. He explained how his mother had worked for the NHS for years but hadn't been offered all of the help she needed to live comfortably.

At the beginning of this book I said that music can be three important things: a celebration, a way of talking about oppression and a type of resistance. 'Black' is all three of these things at the same time. It's angry (look at all the swearing), but it's also poetic. It says that black is beautiful but painful. It's a fight against racism that makes you think.

*

When Lord Kitchener was dreaming of London in 1948, it would have been hard to believe that the children and grandchildren of immigrants like him could end up taking the stage in front of millions to deliver messages of hope and criticism, all mixed up together in rap and piano. This book began just after the Second World War, focusing on the arrival of black West Indians to the UK – people whose ancestors were originally taken from parts of west Africa as slaves. The journey of these groups has not been easy. We have seen how Windrush immigrants suffered and struggled to make a home in Britain, raising families who would continue to feel the effects of racial prejudice and structural racism to this day.

As recently as 2018, it was revealed that at least eighty-three people had been deported by the UK government even though they should have had legal rights to live and work in this country. Many of these people were black West Indians from the Windrush generation who were either born here or arrived legally before immigration laws changed in the 1970s. They had spent their lives in the UK, only to be kicked out of the only place they'd ever known as home. The government has since apologised for what happened, but that doesn't change the fact that many black British people, all the way into the twenty-first century, have been made to feel unwelcome in Britain. Or, at least, well aware of how it feels to be viewed with suspicion.

Now, it's impossible to predict where the journey will take us next. Maybe Dave, and others like him, will go into politics. Maybe they will inspire a child who will grow up to be the first black British prime minister. Maybe his songs, and all of the songs in this book, will end up being studied at schools and in history exams. Who knows? We're living at such an exciting time, with musicians and artists taking a leading role in inspiring future generations.

And who knows what you will achieve? Every generation is special and every generation has an impact on the world. I want you to remember that. You might not record a hit song or invent a new musical genre, but you will shape the future, just by wearing what you wear and listening to what you listen to. Young people push culture forward by embracing new ideas.

Think about the stories you are discovering. Really listen to the people making the music you like. Don't just be dragged into whatever is on the radio or social media. Think about the people behind the music, what their lives are like, their history, their struggles, what they are saying and why they are saying it. It's important. Take it seriously.

'Black and Ready'

Jords (2020)

Black lives matter.
Black lives matter.
Black lives matter.
Black lives matter.

You don't always need a book to bring history alive. Sometimes, history comes to life in the world around you, right before your eyes.

In 2020, the whole world saw history happening in real time. It was fast and exciting, and involved people all over the world who were at the forefront of what felt like real change. You've probably heard of George Floyd. George Floyd was a black American man who was killed by the police, when an officer knelt on his neck for over nine minutes. The incident was filmed on a phone and the video travelled all over the world, shocking millions of people. Suddenly, the full extent of police brutality against black Americans had been revealed. This is nothing new. Black communities in the USA have been the victims of police violence for many years. But something about the horror of George Floyd's death ignited the fires of change.

Soon, all over the world, protests were being held in the name of not only George Floyd but other victims of police brutality as well. Before long, these protests became a global movement in the name of Black Lives Matter, with millions of people taking to the streets to show their support against racism.

Other changes started happening too.

Statues of racist figures from history were taken down from their plinths and pedestals. In the UK, this included a statue of someone called Edward Colston in Bristol, where the bus boycott helped improve race relations back in the 1960s. Edward Colston was a British businessman and slave trader who was responsible for the transportation of many Africans in the late 1600s. Here 'transportation' means being forced to get on board ships that sailed across the oceans, kept in unthinkably bad conditions, only to be sold into slavery at the end of the journey – if you survived. His statue was originally installed in 1895 and was toppled in 2020. It lasted for 125 years, despite people campaigning for it to be removed since the 1990s.

It sounds obvious to say that Black Lives Matter, because all life matters. The reason it is important to highlight black lives in this way and to recognise the truth of these words is that, for many years, the world has operated in a way that suggests that black lives don't matter as much as white lives do. I ask you, is that what you think?

In Britain, Black Lives Matter put the focus on black communities who have suffered racism for decades and continue to do so. As you have seen in this book, these aren't new problems, and they affect every generation. They also aren't and shouldn't be problems for black people to solve alone. They are not of our making, they are problems for all of us to solve together.

'Black and Ready' is the sound of modern resistance against racism. You can even hear the phrase 'Black Lives Matter' being chanted in the background, almost like you are at a real protest in the streets. The song talks about what racism feels like in the twenty-first century: how opportunities for black people are being limited by invisible glass ceilings, how black kids are getting stopped and searched when they are running for the bus, how black people are being killed in the USA for no reason, how black people get attacked on housing estates, how black history doesn't even exist in schools . . . I could go on.

I hope that this book has helped open your eyes to modern black British history, while explaining why there is still a need for anti-racism today. Jords explains that it is hard for black people to trust a system that has been oppressive in so many different ways, but I'd like to be hopeful that we can trust ourselves and each other to do what is right, and step towards a better, brighter future.

Some of the earliest artists in this book came to Britain looking for a new life and a new place to call home. They carried their joy, hope and pain with them in music and songs. If I had a time machine, it would be amazing to play some of the later songs we have heard to some of the musicians who came earlier. What would Lord Kitchener make of Stormzy's lyrics about black pride? What words of advice would Winifred Atwell have about Dave's piano playing? This is what makes music so special. It has the ability to not only carry stories throughout history but also help build towards a better future, growing like a tree with deep roots below and a spreading canopy of glorious, green leaves above.

I'm going to finish up now. But this isn't the end. It's just a powerful place to pause our journey. The one thing we can be sure of is that being black and British is complicated and has often been difficult, but it is ultimately something we can and should all celebrate. This is a truth that music continues to reveal in all sorts of beautiful ways. I hope that this book has shown you that black British history is important for everyone, full of stories of joy and pain, creativity and struggle, uniting communities across the world from one generation to the next – hopefully towards a future of harmony, understanding and, of course, truth.

Acknowledgements

First of all, I have to give a huge wave of recognition to every musician and artist featured in this book. For as long as I can remember, my life has danced to a soundtrack of incredible music. I will always be grateful to have enjoyed the work of so many talented musicians – and there are many more to mention who I couldn't fit in these pages.

Next, a huge thanks goes to Ngadi Smart. I love books with pictures and it's a privilege to have such powerful images alongside my words. Thank you for bringing it all to life. It's amazing.

There are lots of people who are involved in the making of a book and this paragraph is dedicated to them. Thank you to everyone at Faber who helped to bring this book to life. A special thanks goes to Eleanor Rees and to Leah Thaxton, a truly wonderful and enthusiastic editor.

Next, my family. I thank my parents for letting me explore a whole world of music and my excellent big sisters for letting me loose on their music collection when I was growing up.

None of this would be possible without the guidance of my brilliant wife, Sophie, who shares my love of music. And of course, big up my two sons, Finlay and Blake (who have a great taste in music already).

A huge bow for my agent, Sarah Such of Sarah Such Literary Agency, who has always believed in me and my ideas. It means everything to have that kind of support so that books like this can come to life. Thank you.

And finally, thank YOU, whoever you are, reading this right now. If you've got this far you've probably read the rest of the book and it means more than you will ever know to have your support. Without every kind word, every comment on social media, and every turned page, this book wouldn't mean what it does. So thank you. I've fully enjoyed making *Musical Truth* happen and I hope that you too have enjoyed the journey.